Hell

Part 5

Daisy Charles

Hell: Part 5

Contents

Introduction

This is the 5th book in the *Hell* series. If you're not familiar with these here *Hell* books, I can explain what they're all about. In late 2019, I developed a horrible health condition. It was, literally, destroying my life. Some wise colleagues of mine suggested trying active imagination in order to see what role my psyche might be playing in perpetuating this problem. Active Imagination is, essentially, using art in order to communicate with your unconscious – it's something Carl Jung came up with, and it's something I encourage my clients to do in my own psychotherapy practice. The *Hell* series of books is the result of those active imagination exercises.

By the time I wrote this book, the health condition had improved significantly. Who knows? Maybe talking to my unconscious helped some. That said, I still can't relax all-the-way, because there's no guarantee it won't come back. (Sorry for the confusing double negative there).

Because things had gotten better, my mind had more freedom than previously to explore all kinds of things – this book is the result of that exploration. You get to see me take a look at stuff like dreams, childhood memories, my grapplings with how to define my spirituality, and my relationship with my distant ancestors. See, at the end of *Hell: Part 4*, some characters had urged me to use art in order to heal my ancestral traumas. That's what a large part of this book is about.

The characters are me (the girl with the long, blond hair), Jesus (the guy with the mustache and the hat), Chief Running Dog (the guy who wears glasses), Timmy (the bald guy), and Bobby (the heavyset guy with the mustache). These guys are characters from my graphic novels, who kindly offered to be a part of this journey into my psyche. The people who show up on the TV, as well as the dog and the bear, are parts of my unconscious.

I don't think there's much else you need to know about this. Well, I guess one thing I could say is, whereas *Hell* 1, 2, and 3, have a continuous narrative structure, *Hell* 4 and 5 are more like series of vignettes.

As usual, I have a notes section at the end of the book, which will come in handy if you have any questions about it. Enjoy!

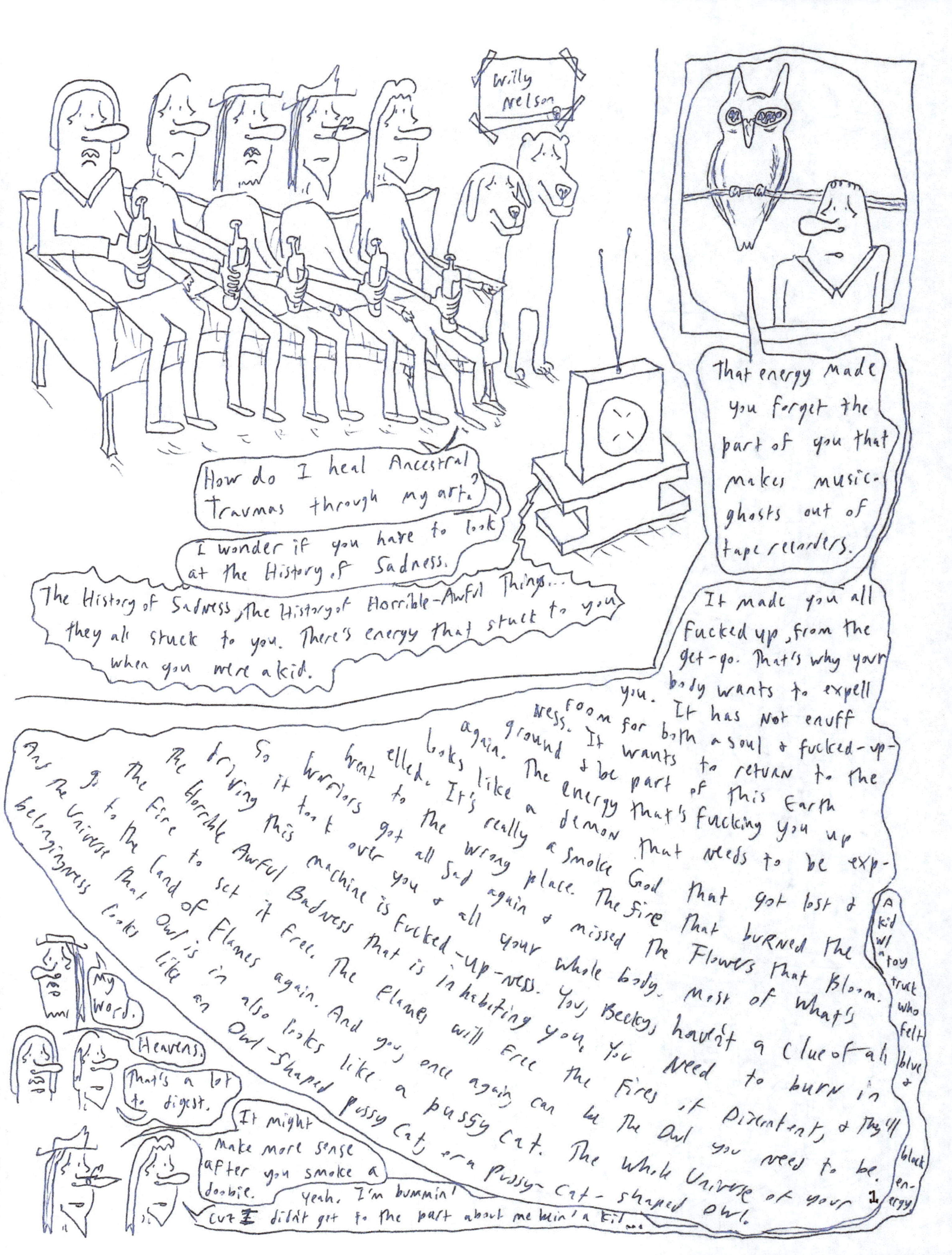

Willy Nelson
How do I heal Ancestral Traumas through my art?
I wonder if you have to look at the History of Sadness.
The History of Sadness, The History of Horrible-Awful Things... they all stuck to you. There's energy that stuck to you when you were a kid.
that energy made you forget the part of you that makes music-ghosts out of tape recorders.
It made you all fucked up, from the get-go. That's why your body wants to expell you. It has Not enuff room for both a soul & fucked-up-ness. It wants to return to the ground & be part of this Earth again. The energy that's fucking you up looks like a demon. It's really a smoke God that got lost & missed the wrong place. The fire that burned the whole body. The Flowers that Bloom. Most of what's... you, Beckys, haven't a clue of all you need to burn in Fires of Discontent, & they'll... The Owl you need to be. The whole Universe of your shaped Owl!
So it went to the warriors to... went elled. It took over you & all your, got all sad again & missed The Fire. The horrible Awful Badness that is inhabiting you, driving this machine, is fucked-up-ness. The Fire to set it free. The flames will Free the flames again. And you, once again, can be The Owl. And to the Universe that Owl is also looks like an Owl-Shaped Pussy Cat, or a Pussy-Cat-shaped Owl. ...the land of Flames... belongingness looks like an Owl...
My Word.
Heavens.
That's a lot to digest.
It might make more sense after you smoke a doobie.
Yeah. I'm bummin' cuz I didn't get to the part about me bein' a Kid...
A kid w/ a toy truck who felt blue & black energy
1.

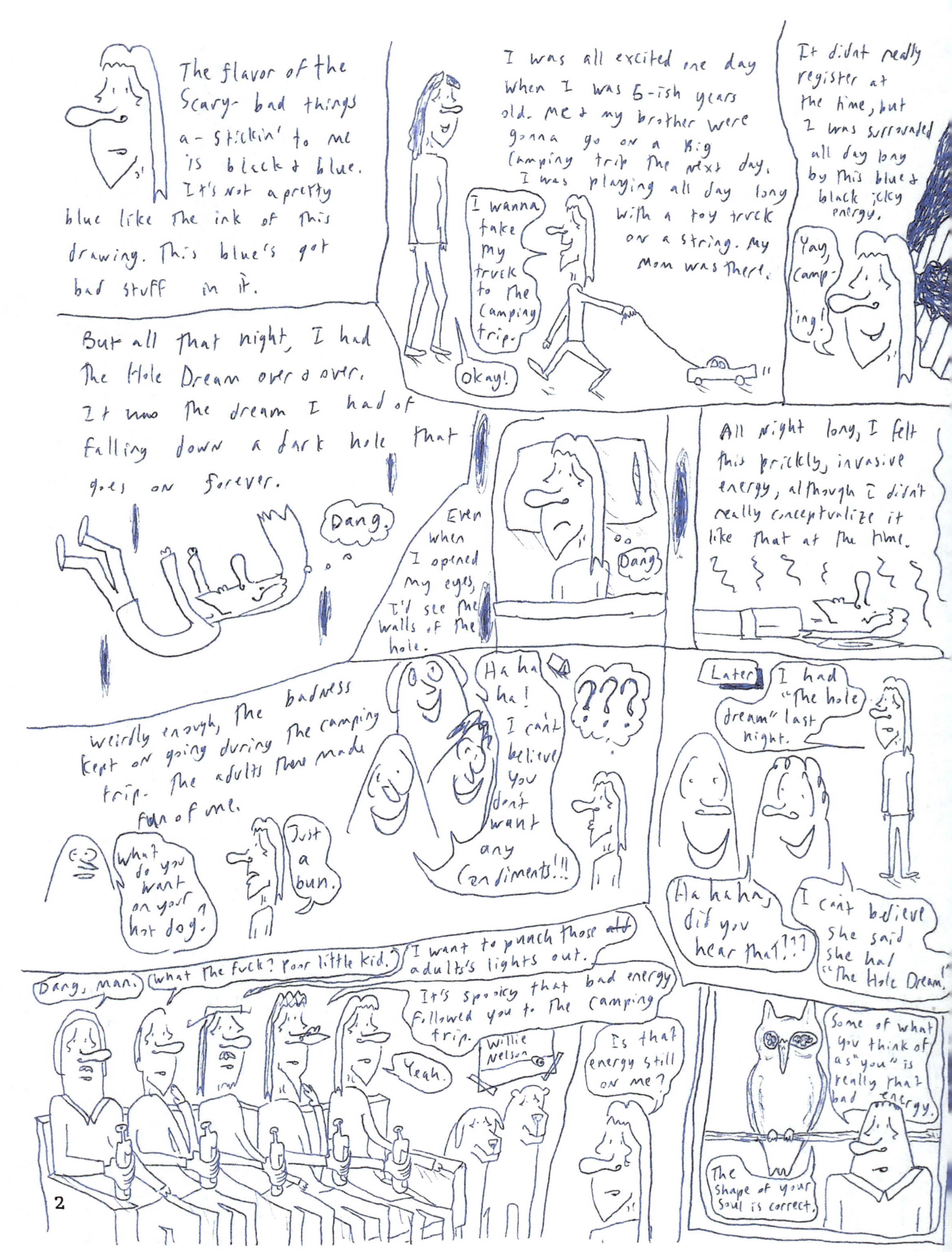

The flavor of the scary-bad things a-stickin' to me is black & blue. It's not a pretty blue like the ink of this drawing. This blue's got bad stuff in it.
I was all excited one day when I was 5-ish years old. Me & my brother were gonna go on a big camping trip the next day. I was playing all day long with a toy truck on a string. My mom was there.
I wanna take my truck to the camping trip.
Okay!
It didn't really register at the time, but I was surrounded all day long by this blue & black icky energy.
Yay, camping!
But all that night, I had the Hole Dream over & over. It was the dream I had of falling down a dark hole that goes on forever.
Dang.
Even when I opened my eyes, I'd see the walls of the hole.
Dang
All night long, I felt this prickly, invasive energy, although I didn't really conceptualize it like that at the time.
Weirdly enough, the badness kept on going during the camping trip. The adults there made fun of me.
What do you want on your hot dog?
Just a bun.
Ha ha ha! I can't believe you don't want any condiments!!!
???
Later I had "The hole dream" last night.
Ha ha ha, did you hear that?!!
I can't believe she said she had "The Hole Dream"!
Dang, man.
What the fuck? Poor little kid.
I want to punch those adults's lights out.
It's spooky that bad energy followed you to the camping trip.
Willie Nelson
Yeah.
Is that energy still on me?
Some of what you think of as "you" is really that bad energy.
The shape of your soul is correct.

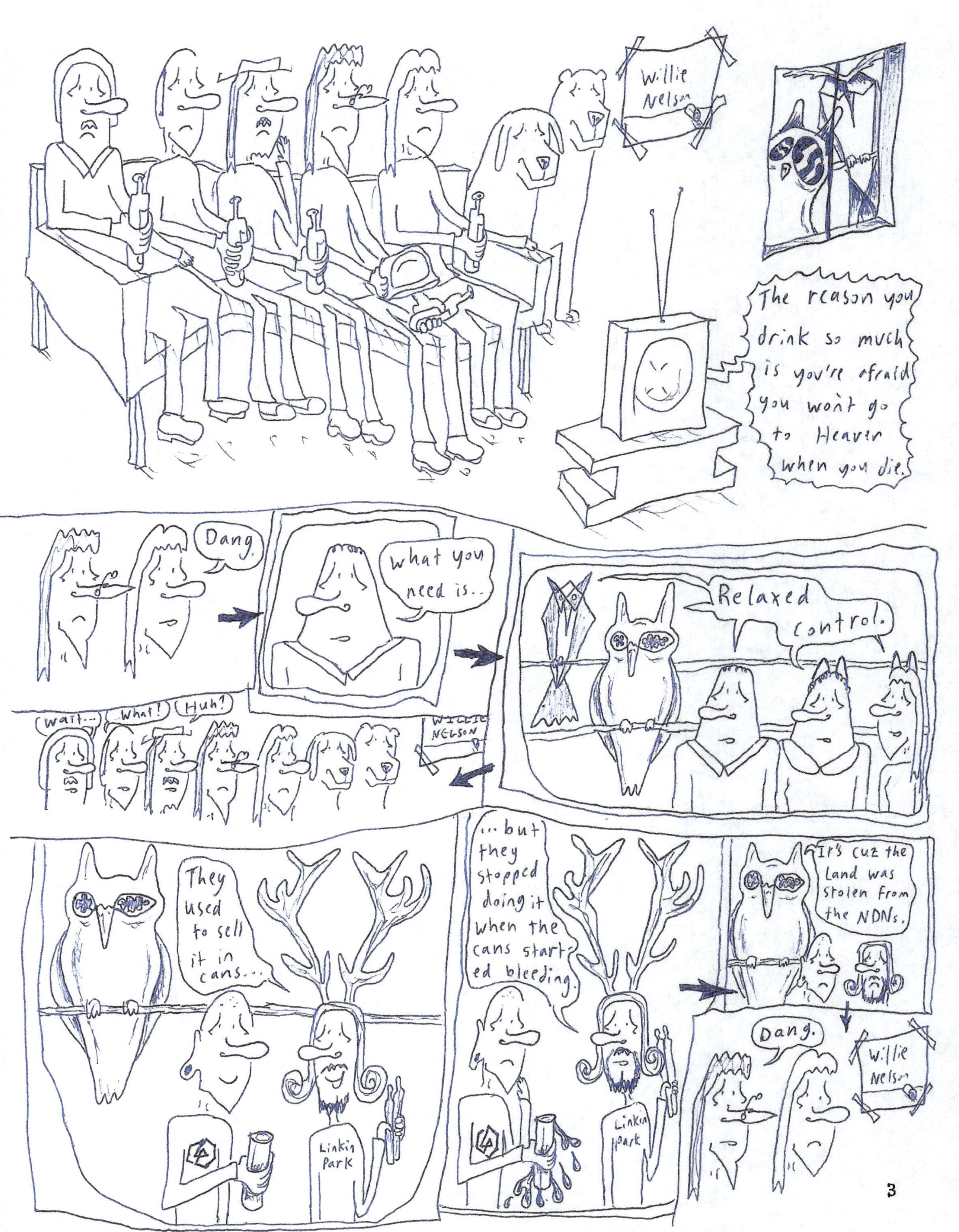

Willie Nelson
The reason you drink so much is you're afraid you won't go to Heaven when you die.
Dang.
what you need is...
Relaxed control.
wait... What! Huh!
WILLIE NELSON
They used to sell it in cans...
Linkin Park
...but they stopped doing it when the cans started bleeding.
Linkin Park
It's cuz the land was stolen from the NDNs.
Dang.
Willie Nelson

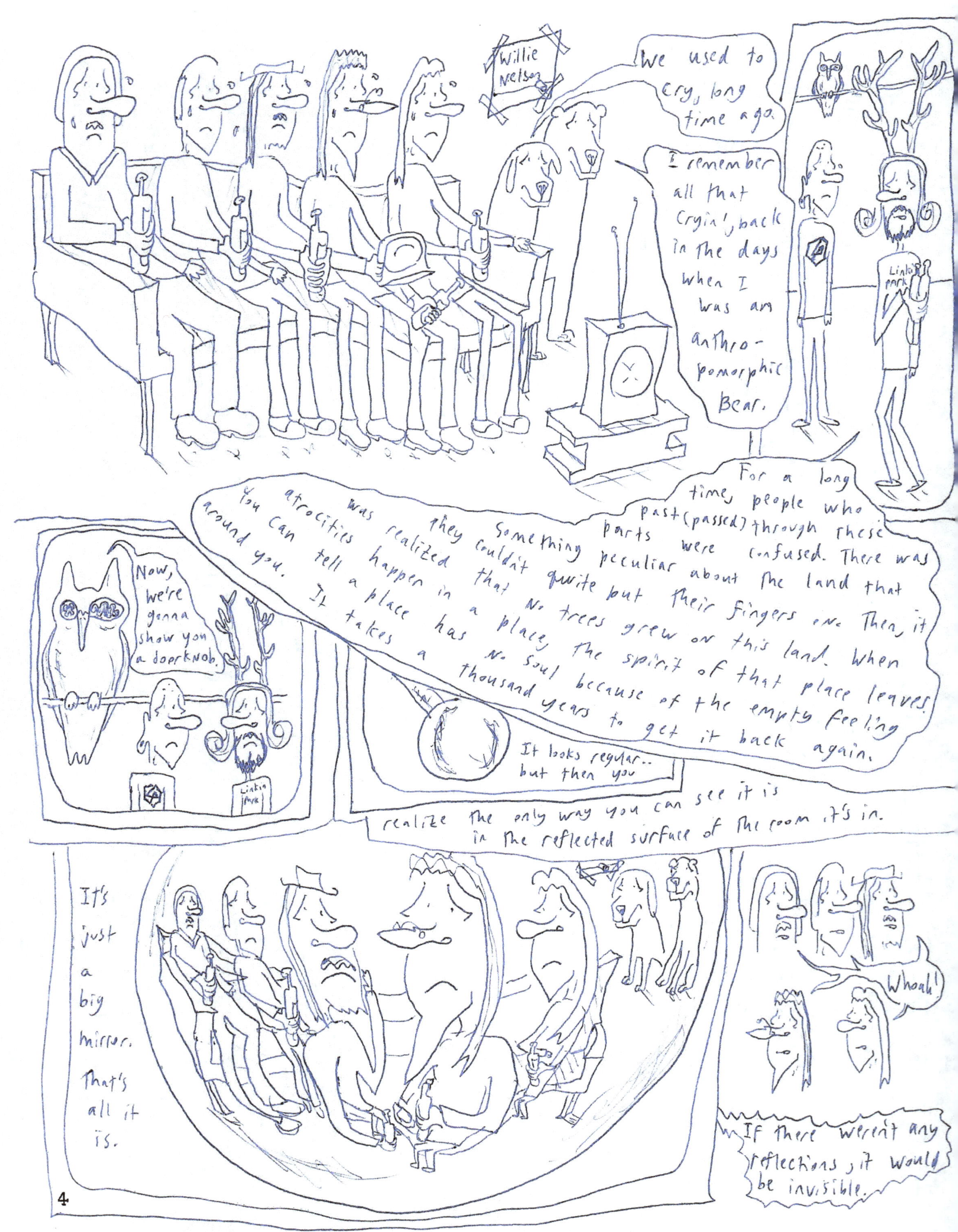

Willie Nelson
We used to cry, long time ago.
I remember all that cryin', back in the days when I was an anthropomorphic Bear.
Linkin Park
For a long time, people who past (passed) through these parts were confused. There was something peculiar about the land that they couldn't quite put their fingers on. Then, it was realized that no trees grew on this land. When atrocities happen in a place, the spirit of that place leaves. You can tell a place has no soul because of the empty feeling around you. It takes a thousand years to get it back again.
Now, we're gonna show you a doorknob.
Linkin Park
It looks regular.. but then you realize the only way you can see it is in the reflected surface of the room it's in.
It's just a big mirror. That's all it is.
Whoah!
If there weren't any reflections, it would be invisible.

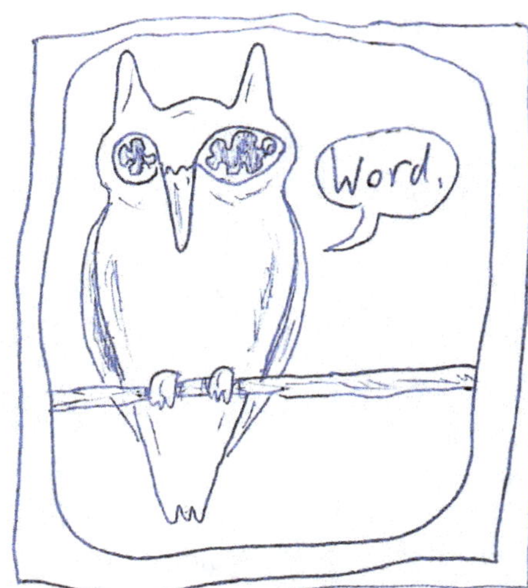

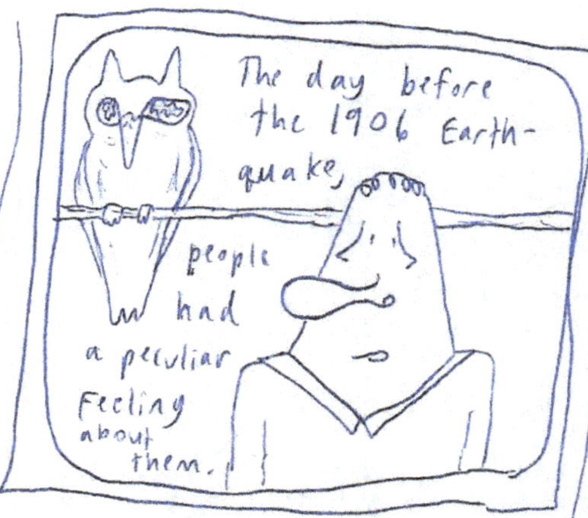

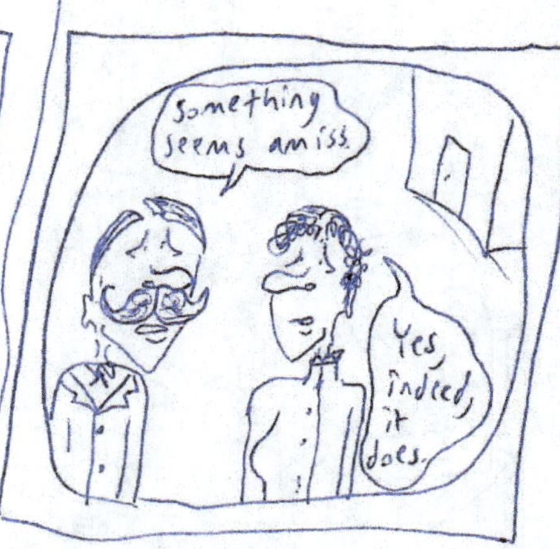

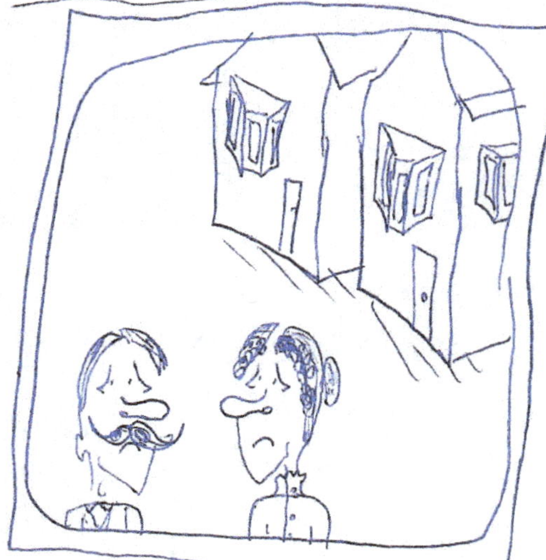

What they didn't realize was... the spirits of all the buildings had already left because they knew they were gonna burn down soon.

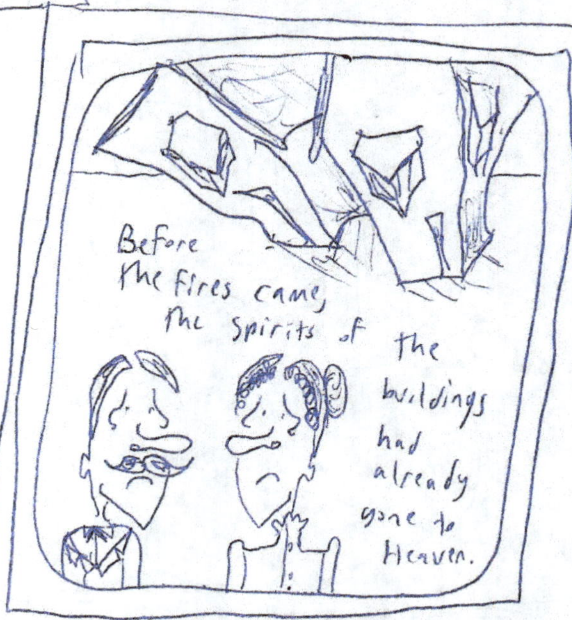

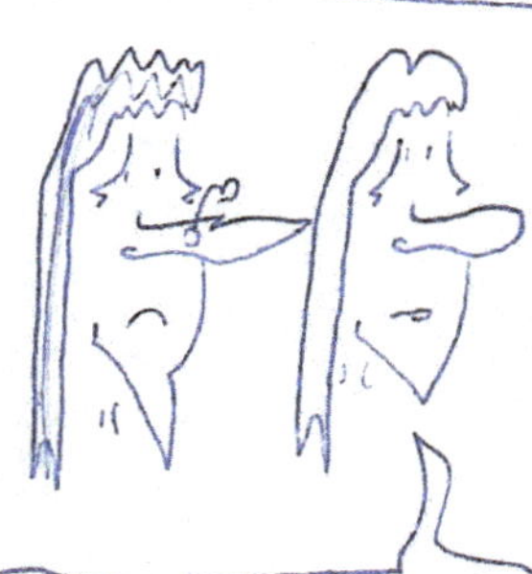

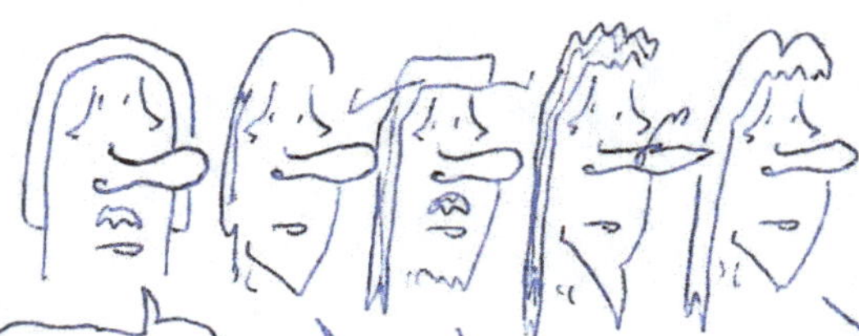

When I go to those places, it feels like empty darkness. It feels black. But I don't understand. When a place or a thing loses its soul, what's the soul of the leftover thing? My brain keeps telling me that EVERYTHING has a soul. Like it's a law of physics or something. What is the soul of something that doesn't have a soul?

Maybe it's the atoms & molecules that make up the thing. Maybe the souls of those are the soul of the thing.

And the lack of a unifying force makes the thing lose coherency. And that's why it feels black.

I once saw a soul-less man during my Biblical days. It freaked me out.

When you cut down a tree to make a house, the house has a house-soul. The tree-soul's gone to Heaven.

This piece of paper has a paper-soul. But it's even better because it has animals on it.

An explanation of why a thing can lose a soul, but have another soul already there.

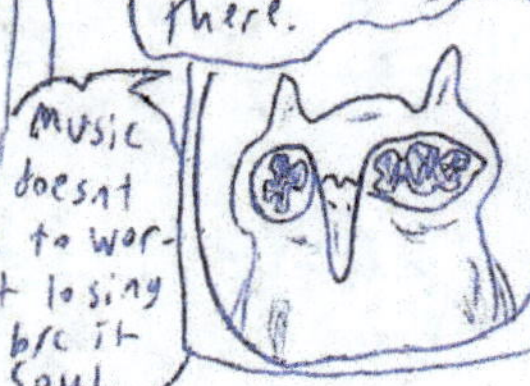

5

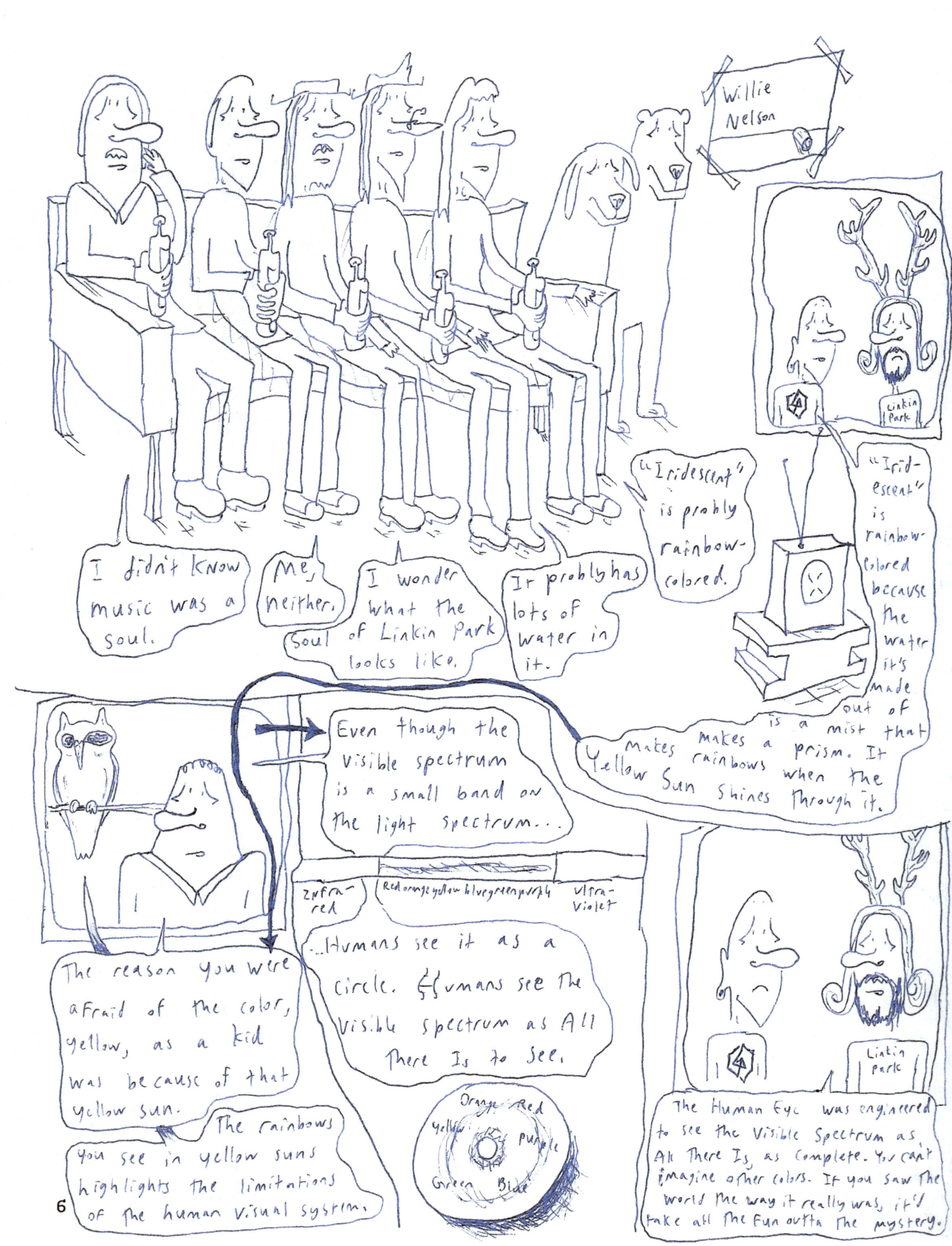

Willie Nelson
Linkin Park
I didn't know music was a soul.
Me, neither.
I wonder what the soul of Linkin Park looks like.
It probly has lots of water in it.
"Iridescent" is probly rainbow-colored.
"Iridescent" is rainbow-colored because the water it's made out of is a mist that makes a prism. It mates rainbows when the Yellow Sun Shines Through it.
Even though the visible spectrum is a small band on the light spectrum...
Infra-red
Red orange yellow blue green purple
Ultra-Violet
...Humans see it as a circle. Humans see the visible spectrum as All There Is to See.
The reason you were afraid of the color, yellow, as a kid was because of that yellow sun.
The rainbows you see in yellow suns highlights the limitations of the human visual system.
Orange Red
Yellow
Purple
Green Blue
Linkin Park
The Human Eye was engineered to see the Visible Spectrum as All There Is, as complete. You can't imagine other colors. If you saw the world the way it really was, it'd take all the fun outta the mystery.

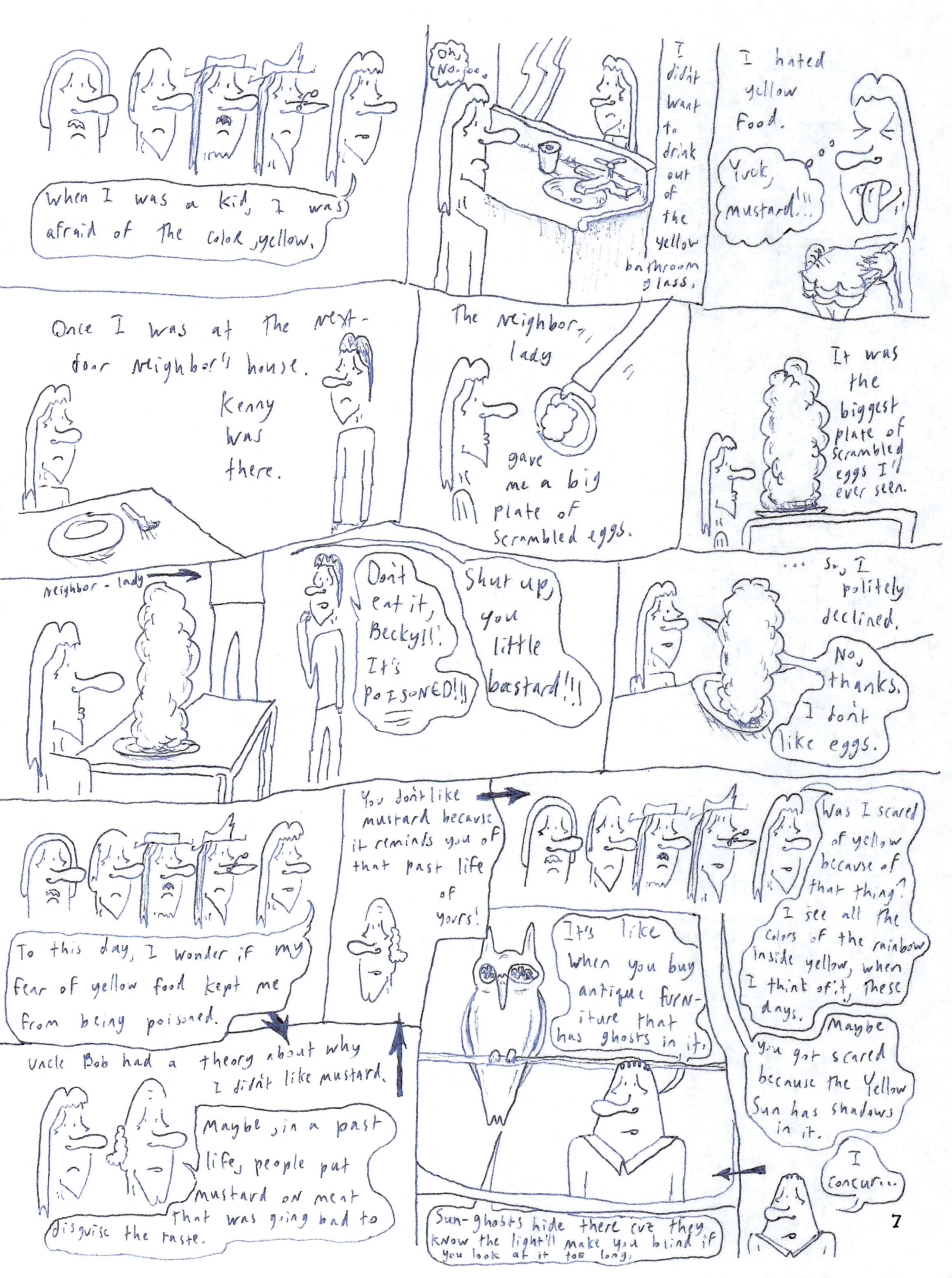

When I was a kid, I was afraid of the color yellow.

Oh, no...oo..
I didn't want to drink out of the yellow bathroom glass.

I hated yellow food.
Yuck, mustard...

Once I was at the next-door neighbor's house. Kenny was there.

The neighbor lady gave me a big plate of scrambled eggs.

It was the biggest plate of scrambled eggs I'd ever seen.

Neighbor - lady
Don't eat it, Becky!! It's POISONED!!!
Shut up, you little bastard!!!

...So, I politely declined.
No, thanks. I don't like eggs.

To this day, I wonder if my fear of yellow food kept me from being poisoned.

You don't like mustard because it reminds you of that past life of yours!

Uncle Bob had a theory about why I didn't like mustard.

Maybe, in a past life, people put mustard on meat that was going bad to disguise the taste.

It's like when you buy antique furniture that has ghosts in it.

Was I scared of yellow because of that thing? I see all the colors of the rainbow inside yellow, when I think of it, these days. Maybe you got scared because the yellow sun has shadows in it.

I concur...

Sun-ghosts hide there cuz they know the light'll make you blind if you look at it too long.

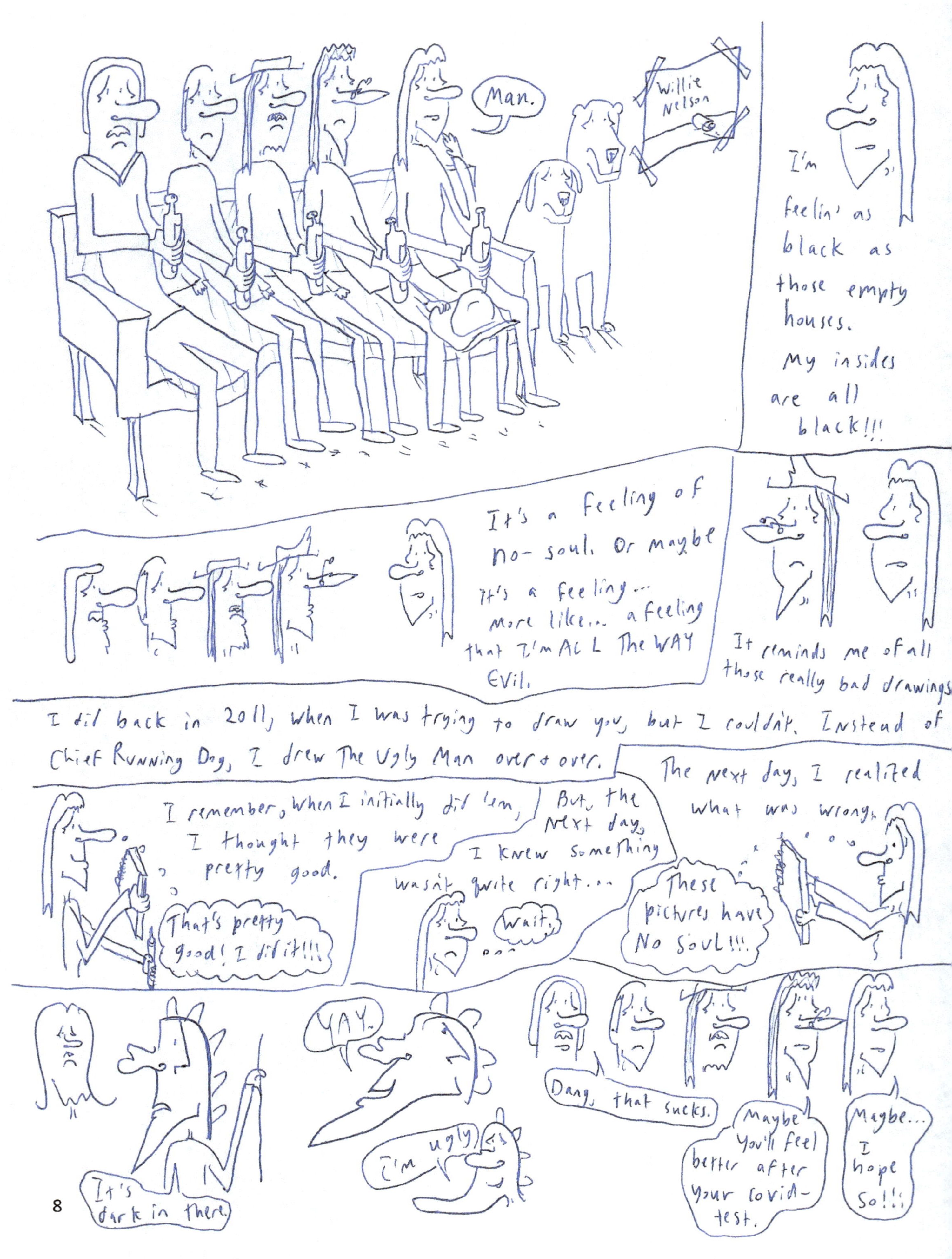

Man.
Willie Nelson
I'm feelin' as black as those empty houses.
My insides are all black!!!
It's a feeling of no-soul. Or maybe it's a feeling... more like... a feeling that I'm ALL THE WAY Evil.
It reminds me of all those really bad drawings
I did back in 2011, when I was trying to draw you, but I couldn't. Instead of Chief Running Dog, I drew The Ugly Man over & over.
I remember, when I initially did 'em, I thought they were pretty good.
That's pretty good! I did it!!!
But, the next day, I knew something wasn't quite right...
Wait,
The next day, I realized what was wrong.
These pictures have No Soul!!!
It's dark in there.
YAY.
I'm ugly
Dang, that sucks.
Maybe you'll feel better after your covid-test.
Maybe... I hope so!!!

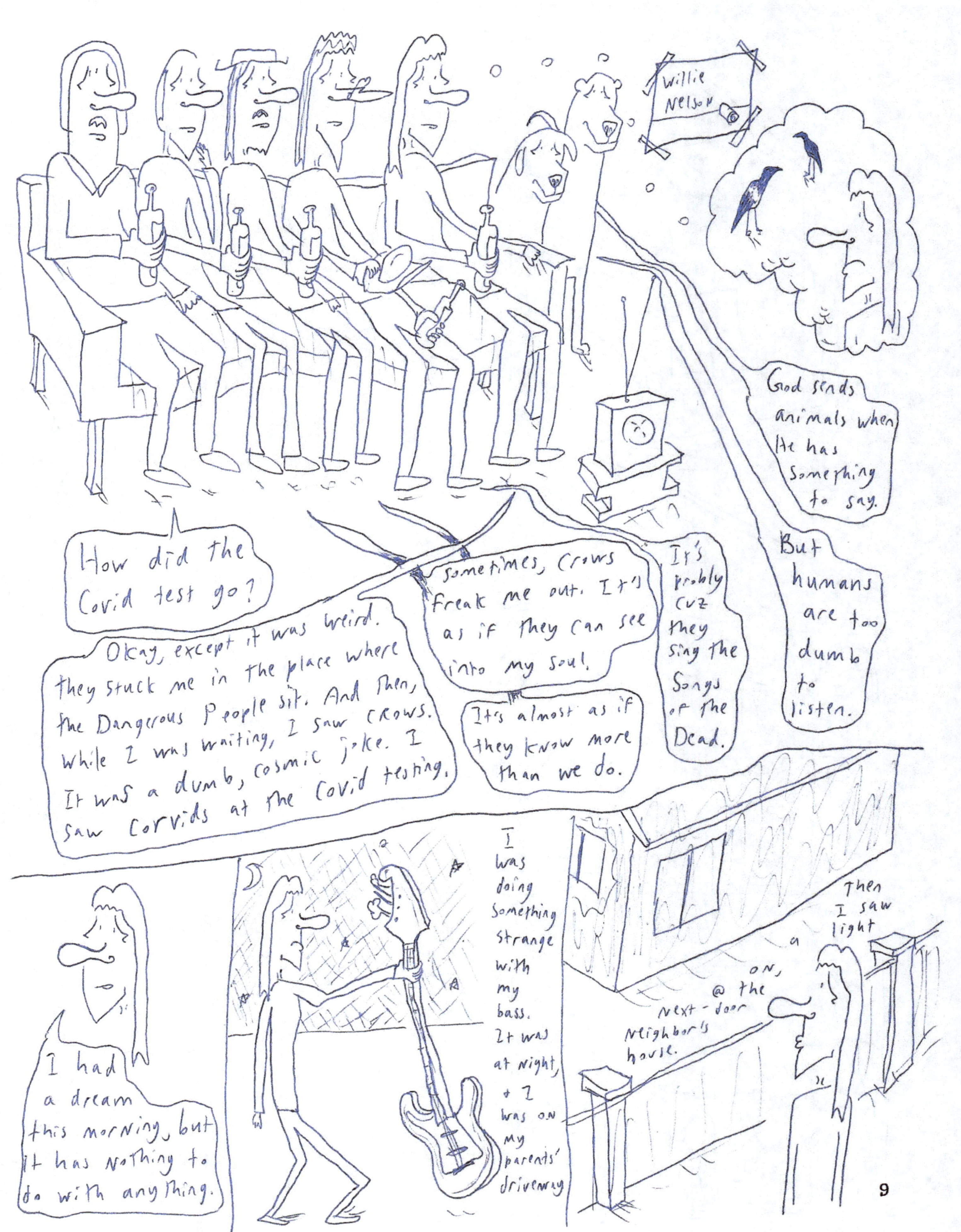

Willie Nelson
God sends animals when He has something to say.
But humans are too dumb to listen.
How did the Covid test go?
Okay, except it was weird. They stuck me in the place where the Dangerous People sit. And then, while I was waiting, I saw crows. It was a dumb, cosmic joke. I saw Corvids at the Covid testing.
Sometimes, crows freak me out. It's as if they can see into my soul.
It's almost as if they know more than we do.
It's probly cuz they sing the songs of the Dead.
I had a dream this morning, but it has nothing to do with anything.
I was doing something strange with my bass. It was at night, & I was on my parents' driveway
Then I saw light
on, @ the next-door Neighbor's house.

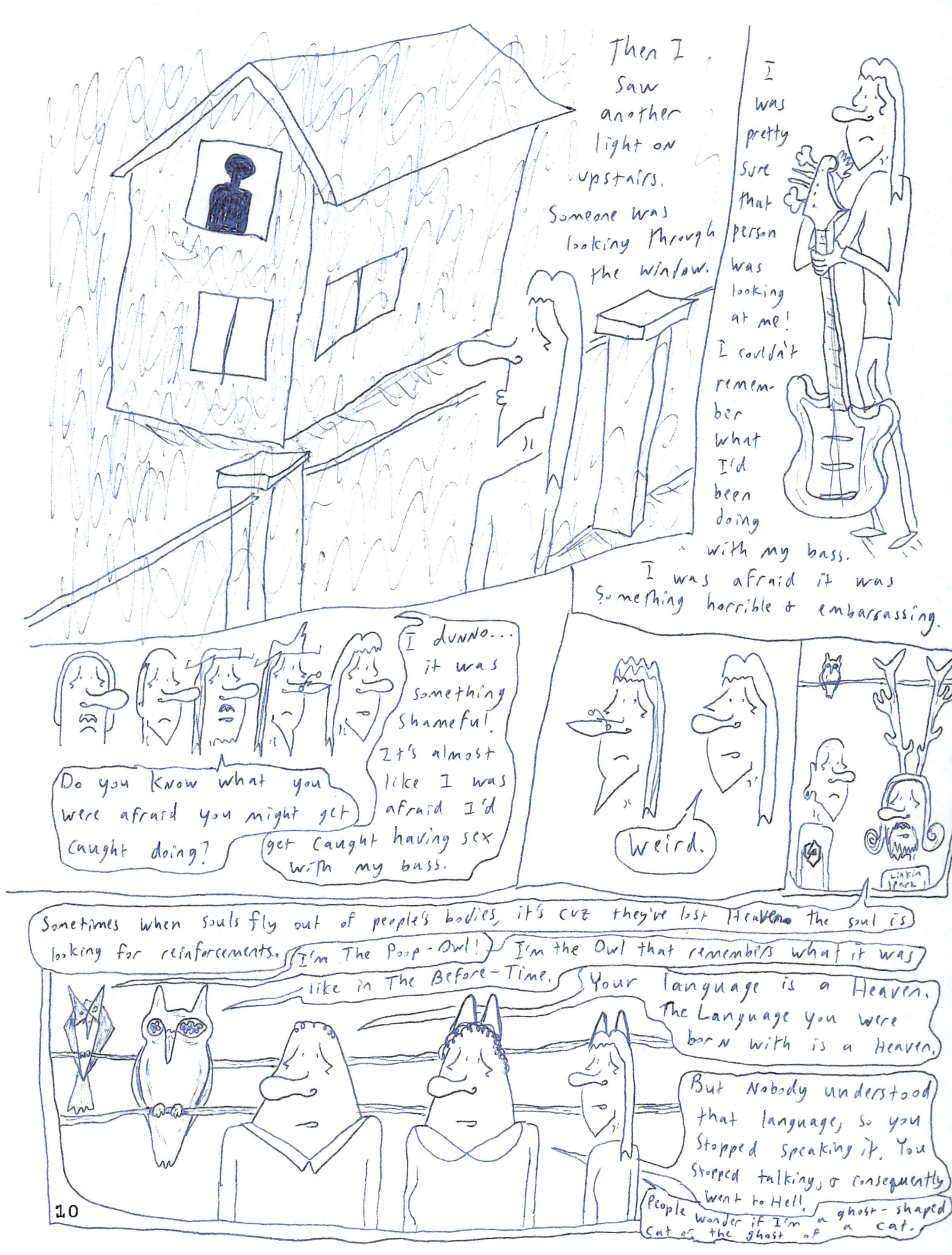

Then I saw another light on upstairs.
Someone was looking through the window.
I was pretty sure that person was looking at me! I couldn't remember what I'd been doing with my bass.
I was afraid it was something horrible & embarrassing.
Do you know what you were afraid you might get caught doing?
I dunno... it was something shameful. It's almost like I was afraid I'd get caught having sex with my bass.
Weird.
Linkin Park
Sometimes when souls fly out of people's bodies, it's cuz they've lost Heaven & the soul is looking for reinforcements.
I'm The Poop-Owl!
I'm the Owl that remembers what it was like in The Before-Time.
Your language is a Heaven. The Language you were born with is a Heaven.
But Nobody understood that language, so you stopped speaking it. You stopped talking, & consequently went to Hell.
People wonder if I'm a ghost-shaped cat or the ghost of a cat.
10

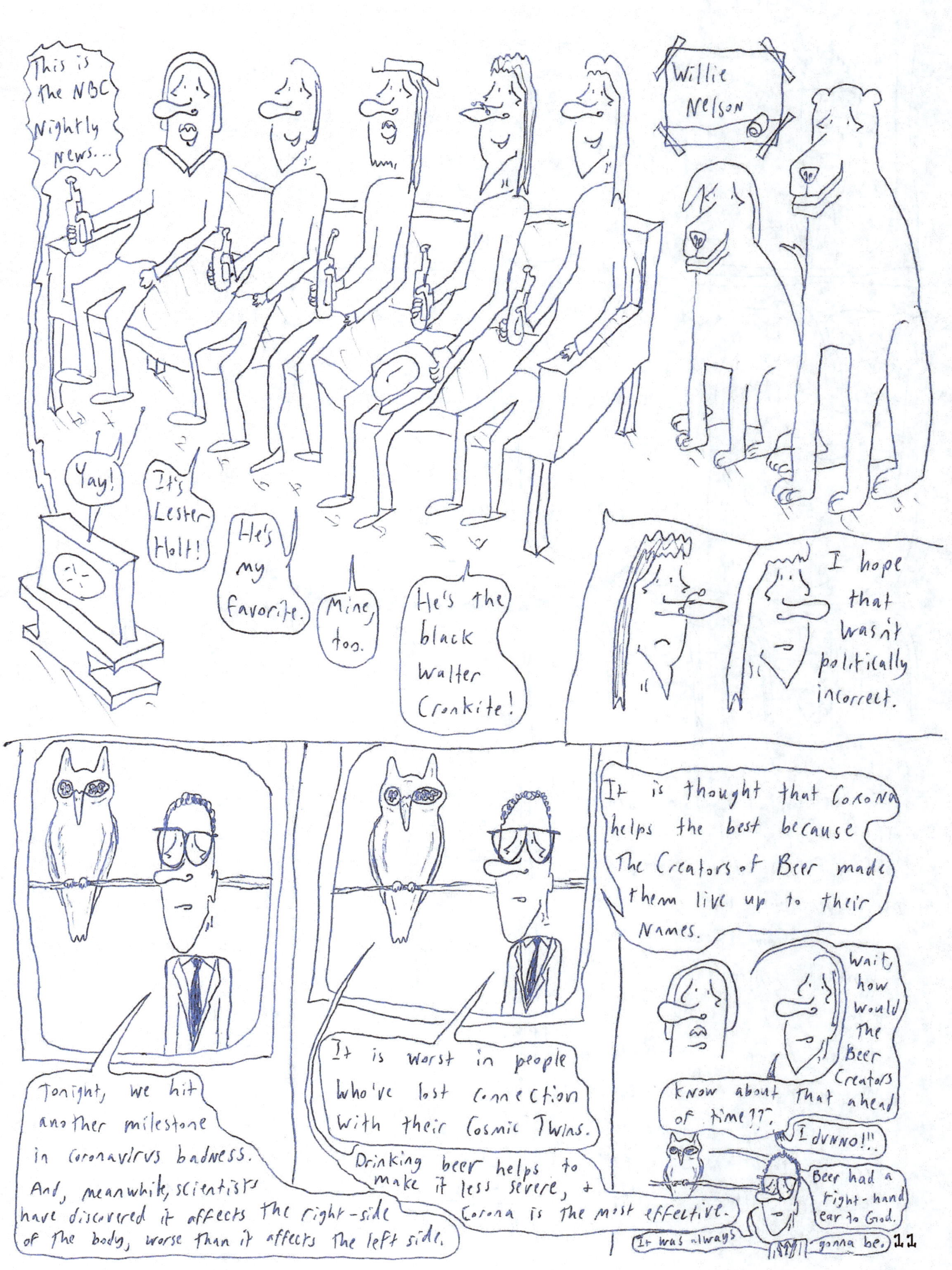

This is the NBC Nightly News...
Yay!
It's Lester Holt!
He's my favorite.
Mine, too.
He's the black Walter Cronkite!
Willie Nelson
I hope that wasn't politically incorrect.
Tonight, we hit another milestone in coronavirus badness. And, meanwhile, scientists have discovered it affects the right-side of the body, worse than it affects the left side.
It is worst in people who've lost connection with their Cosmic Twins.
Drinking beer helps to make it less severe, & Corona is the most effective.
It is thought that Corona helps the best because The Creators of Beer made them live up to their Names.
Wait, how would The Beer Creators know about that ahead of time??
I dunno!!!
Beer had a right-hand ear to God.
It was always gonna be.

11

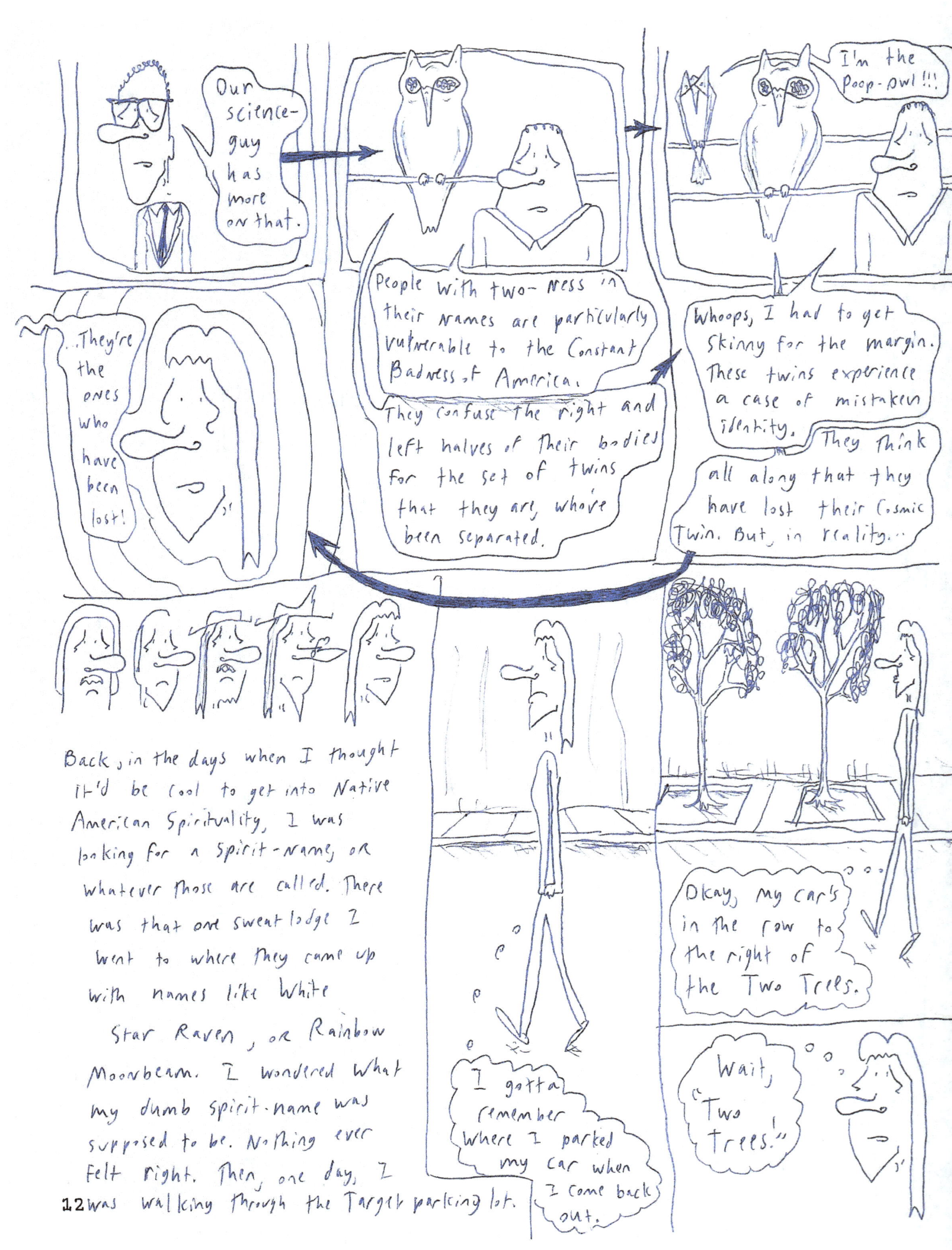

Back, in the days when I thought it'd be cool to get into Native American Spirituality, I was looking for a spirit-name, or whatever those are called. There was that one sweat lodge I went to where they came up with names like White Star Raven, or Rainbow Moonbeam. I wondered what my dumb spirit-name was supposed to be. Nothing ever felt right. Then, one day, I was walking through the Target parking lot.

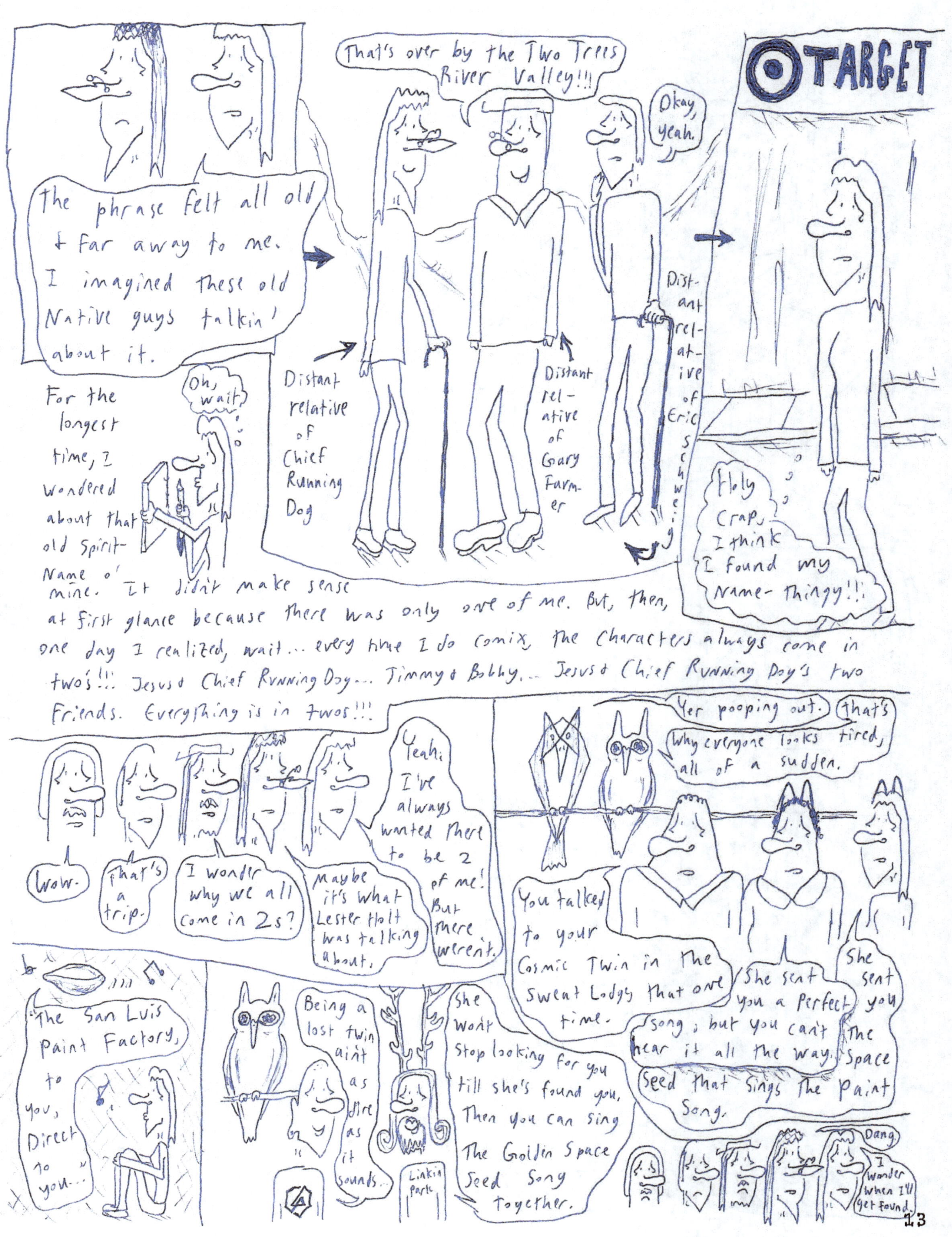

the phrase felt all old & far away to me. I imagined these old Native guys talkin' about it.
That's over by the Two Trees River Valley!!!
Okay, yeah.
TARGET
Oh, wait.
Distant relative of Chief Running Dog
Distant relative of Gary Farmer
Distant relative of Eric Schweig...
For the longest time, I wondered about that old Spirit-Name o' mine. It didn't make sense at first glance because there was only one of me. But, then, one day I realized, wait... every time I do comix, the characters always come in two's!!! Jesus & Chief Running Dog... Jimmy & Bobby... Jesus & Chief Running Dog's two friends. Everything is in twos!!!
Holy Crap, I think I found my Name-Thingy!!!
Wow.
That's a trip.
I wonder why we all come in 2s?
Maybe it's what Lester Holt was talking about.
Yeah, I've always wanted there to be 2 of me! But there weren't.
Yer pooping out. That's why everyone looks tired, all of a sudden.
You talked to your Cosmic Twin in the Sweat Lodge that one time.
She won't stop looking for you till she's found you. Then you can sing the Golden Space Seed Song together.
She sent you a Perfect Song, but you can't hear it all the way.
She sent you The Space Seed that sings the Paint Song.
"The San Luis Paint Factory, to you, Direct to you..."
Being a lost twin ain't as dire as it sounds...
Linkin Park
Dang, I wonder when I'll get found.

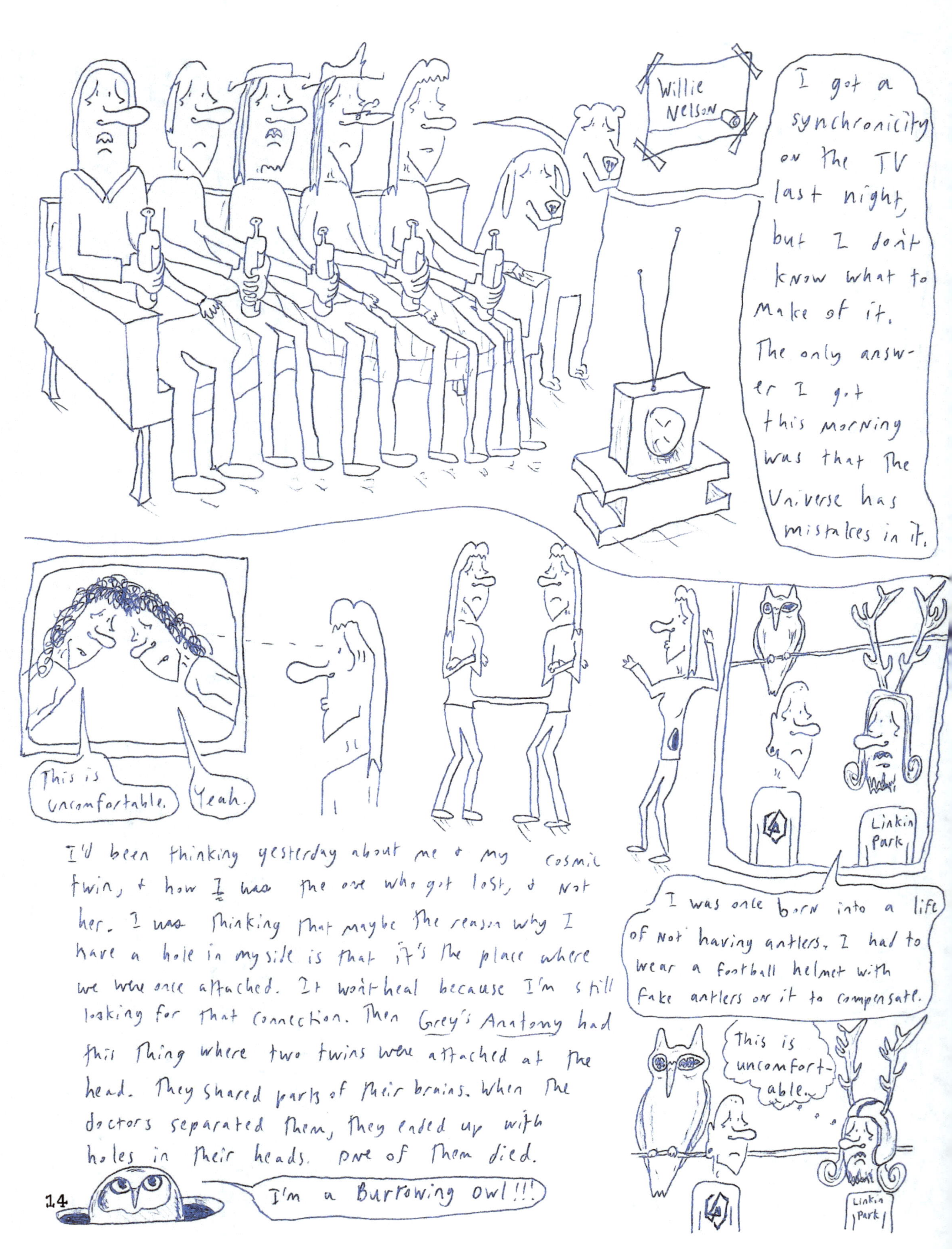

Willie Nelson

I got a synchronicity on the TV last night, but I don't know what to make of it. The only answer I got this morning was that The Universe has mistakes in it.

This is uncomfortable.

Yeah.

I was once born into a life of not having antlers. I had to wear a football helmet with fake antlers on it to compensate.

This is uncomfortable.

Linkin Park

Linkin Park

I've been thinking yesterday about me & my cosmic twin, & how I was the one who got lost, & not her. I was thinking that maybe the reason why I have a hole in my side is that it's the place where we were once attached. It won't heal because I'm still looking for that connection. Then Grey's Anatomy had this thing where two twins were attached at the head. They shared parts of their brains. When the doctors separated them, they ended up with holes in their heads. One of them died.

I'm a Burrowing Owl!!!

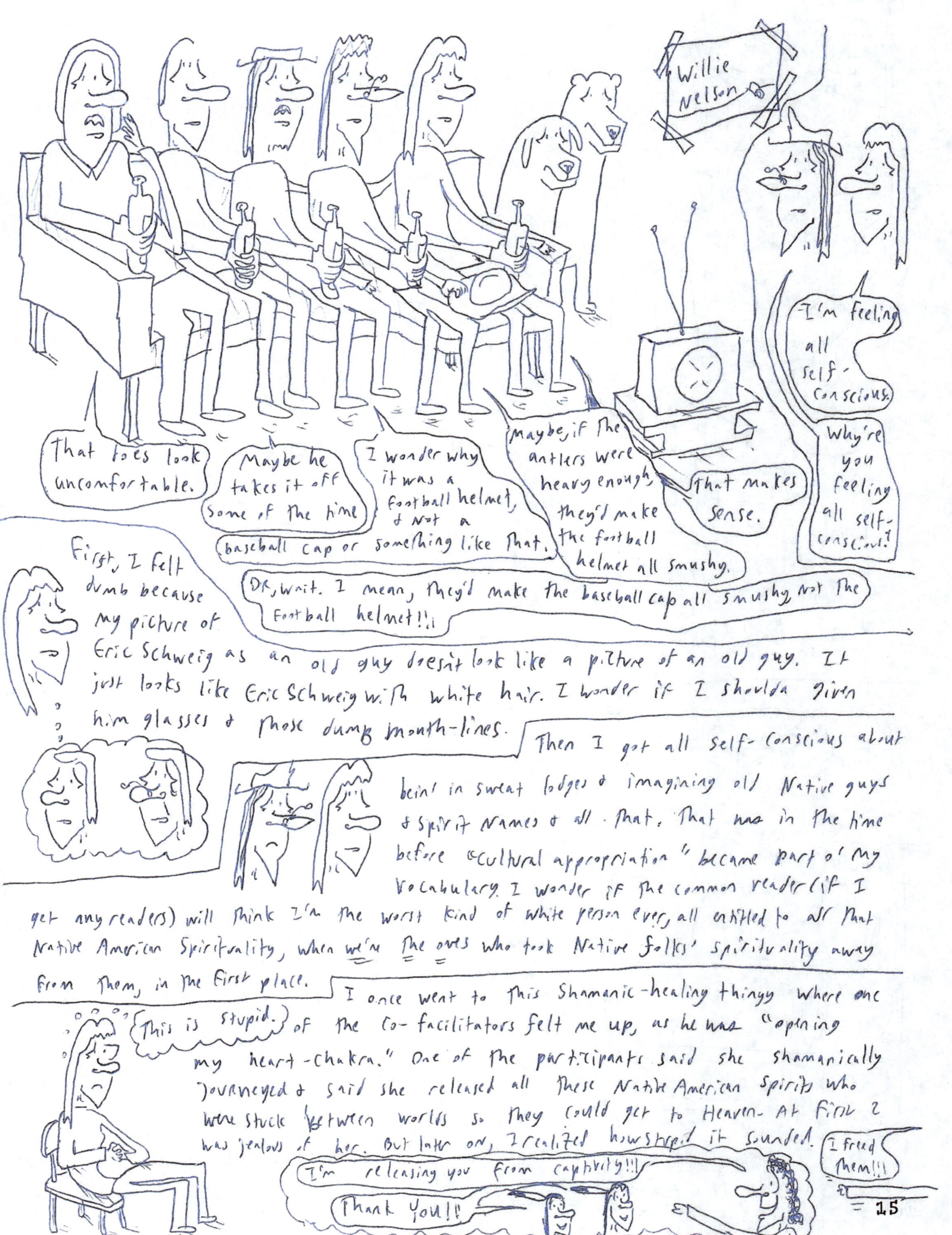

Willie Nelson
I'm feeling all self-conscious.
Why're you feeling all self-conscious?
That toes look uncomfortable.
Maybe he takes it off some of the time
I wonder why it was a football helmet, & not a baseball cap or something like that.
Maybe, if the antlers were heavy enough, they'd make the football helmet all smushy.
That makes sense.
Oh, wait. I mean, they'd make the baseball cap all smushy, not the football helmet!!!
First, I felt dumb because my picture of Eric Schweig as an old guy doesn't look like a picture of an old guy. It just looks like Eric Schweig with white hair. I wonder if I shoulda given him glasses & those dumb mouth-lines.
Then I got all self-conscious about bein' in sweat lodges & imagining old Native guys & spirit names & all. That. That was in the time before "cultural appropriation" became part o' my vocabulary. I wonder if the common reader (if I get any readers) will think I'm the worst kind of white person ever, all entitled to all that Native American spirituality, when we're the ones who took Native folks' spirituality away from them, in the first place.
(This is stupid.)
I once went to this shamanic-healing thingy where one of the co-facilitators felt me up, as he was "opening my heart-chakra." One of the participants said she shamanically journeyed & said she released all these Native American spirits who were stuck between worlds so they could get to Heaven. At first I was jealous of her. But later on, I realized how stupid it sounded.
I'm releasing you from captivity!!!
Thank you!!
I freed them!!!
15

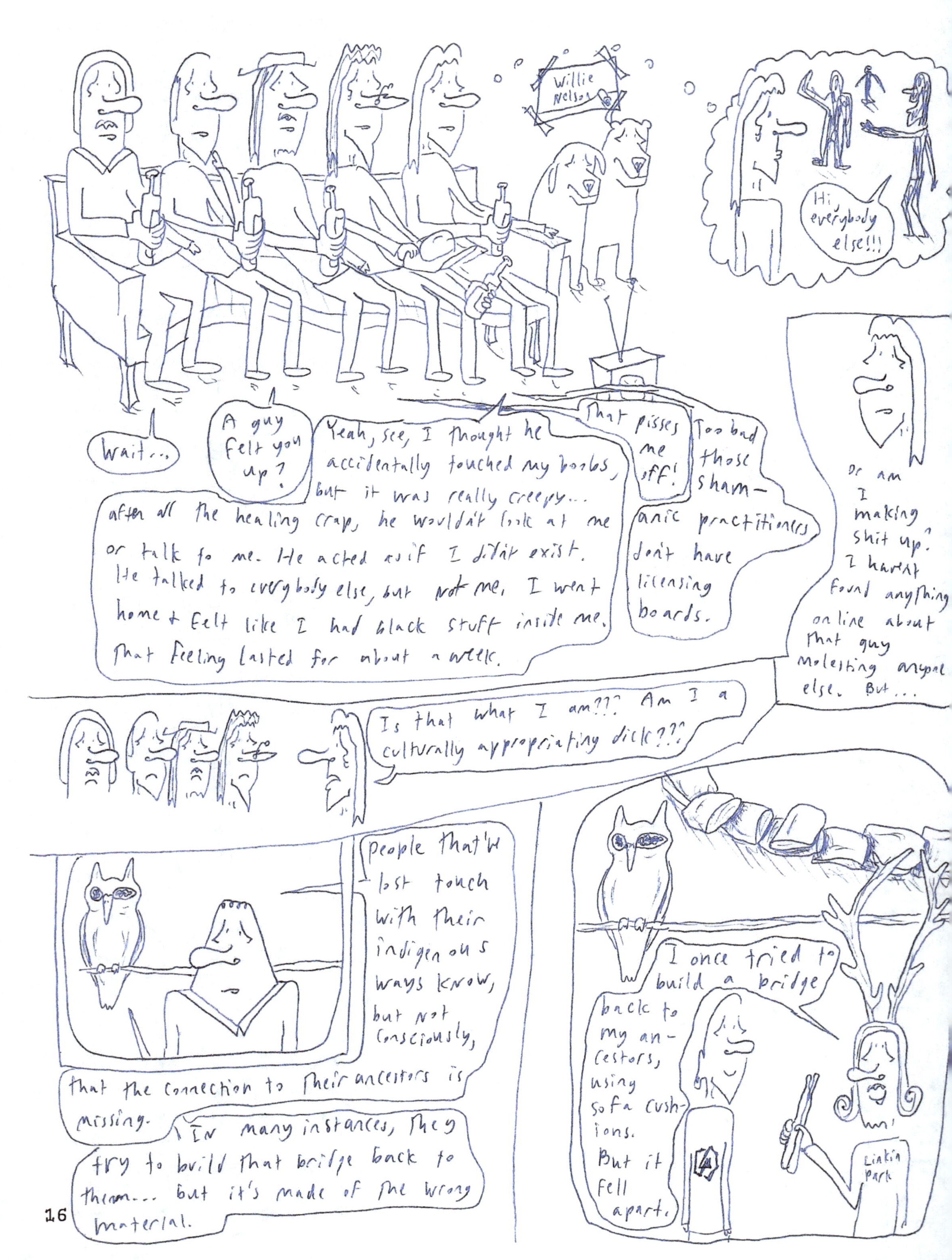

Willie Nelson
Hi everybody else!!!
Wait...
A guy felt you up?
Yeah, see, I thought he accidentally touched my boobs, but it was really creepy... after all the healing crap, he wouldn't look at me or talk to me. He acted as if I didn't exist. He talked to everybody else, but not me. I went home & felt like I had black stuff inside me. That feeling lasted for about a week.
That pisses me off!
Too bad those sham- anic practitioners don't have licensing boards.
Or am I making shit up? I haven't found anything online about that guy molesting anyone else. But...
Is that what I am??? Am I a culturally appropriating dick???
people that've lost touch with their indigenous ways know, but not consciously, that the connection to their ancestors is missing. In many instances, they try to build that bridge back to them... but it's made of the wrong material.
I once tried to build a bridge back to my an- cestors, using sofa cush- ions. But it fell apart.
Linkin Park
16

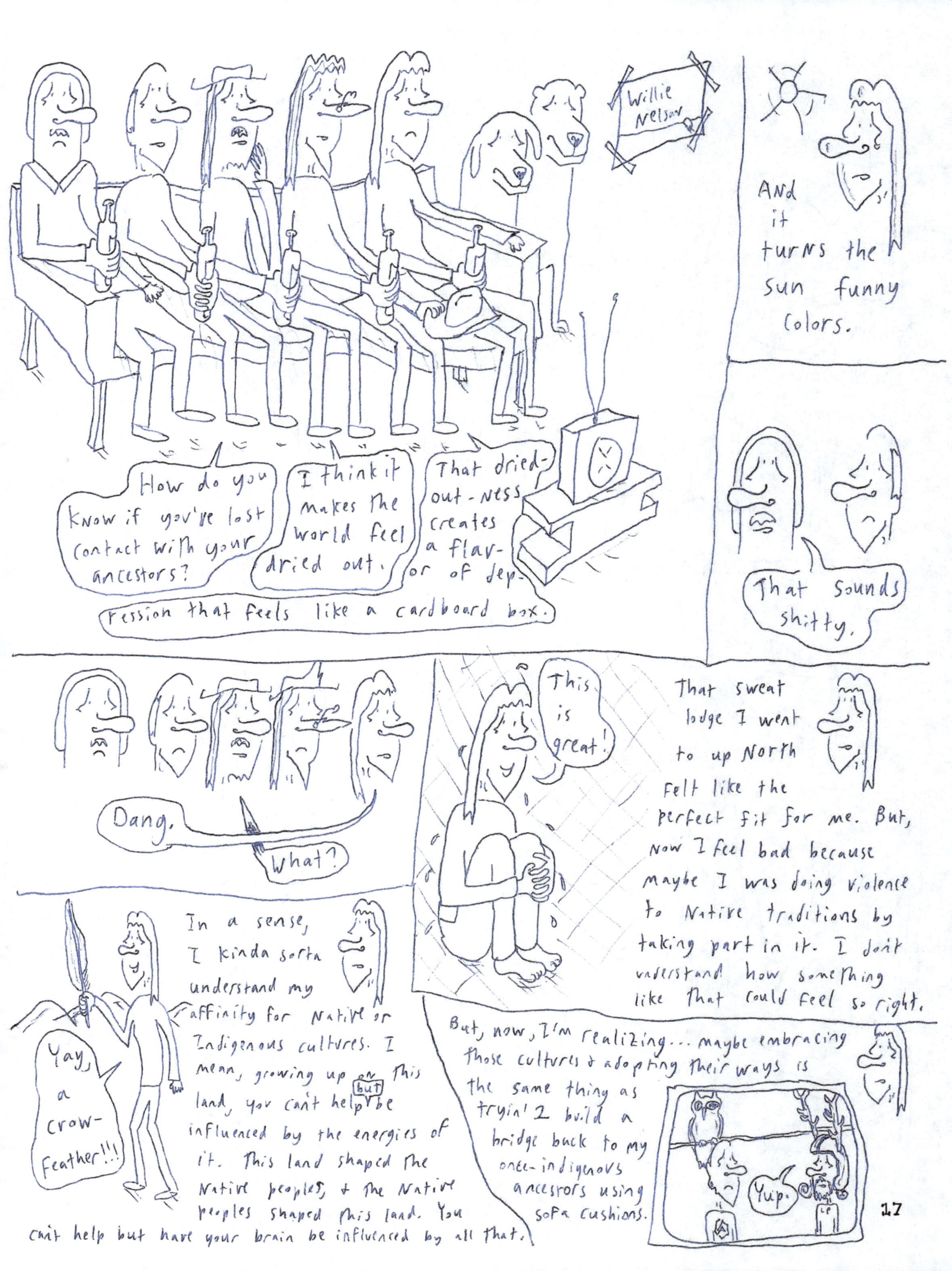

Willie Nelson
AND it turNs the sun funny colors.
How do you know if you've lost contact with your ancestors?
I think it makes the world feel dried out.
That dried-out-ness creates a flav-or of dep-ression that feels like a cardboard box.
That sounds shitty.
Dang.
What?
This is great!
That sweat lodge I went to up North felt like the perfect fit for me. But, now I feel bad because maybe I was doing violence to Native traditions by taking part in it. I don't understand how something like that could feel so right.
In a sense, I kinda sorta understand my affinity for Native or Indigenous cultures. I mean, growing up on this land, you can't help but be influenced by the energies of it. This land shaped the Native peoples, & the Native peoples shaped this land. You can't help but have your brain be influenced by all that.
Yay, a crow-feather!!!
But, now, I'm realizing... maybe embracing those cultures & adopting their ways is the same thing as tryin' 2 build a bridge back to my once-indigenous ancestors using sofa cushions.
Yup.
17

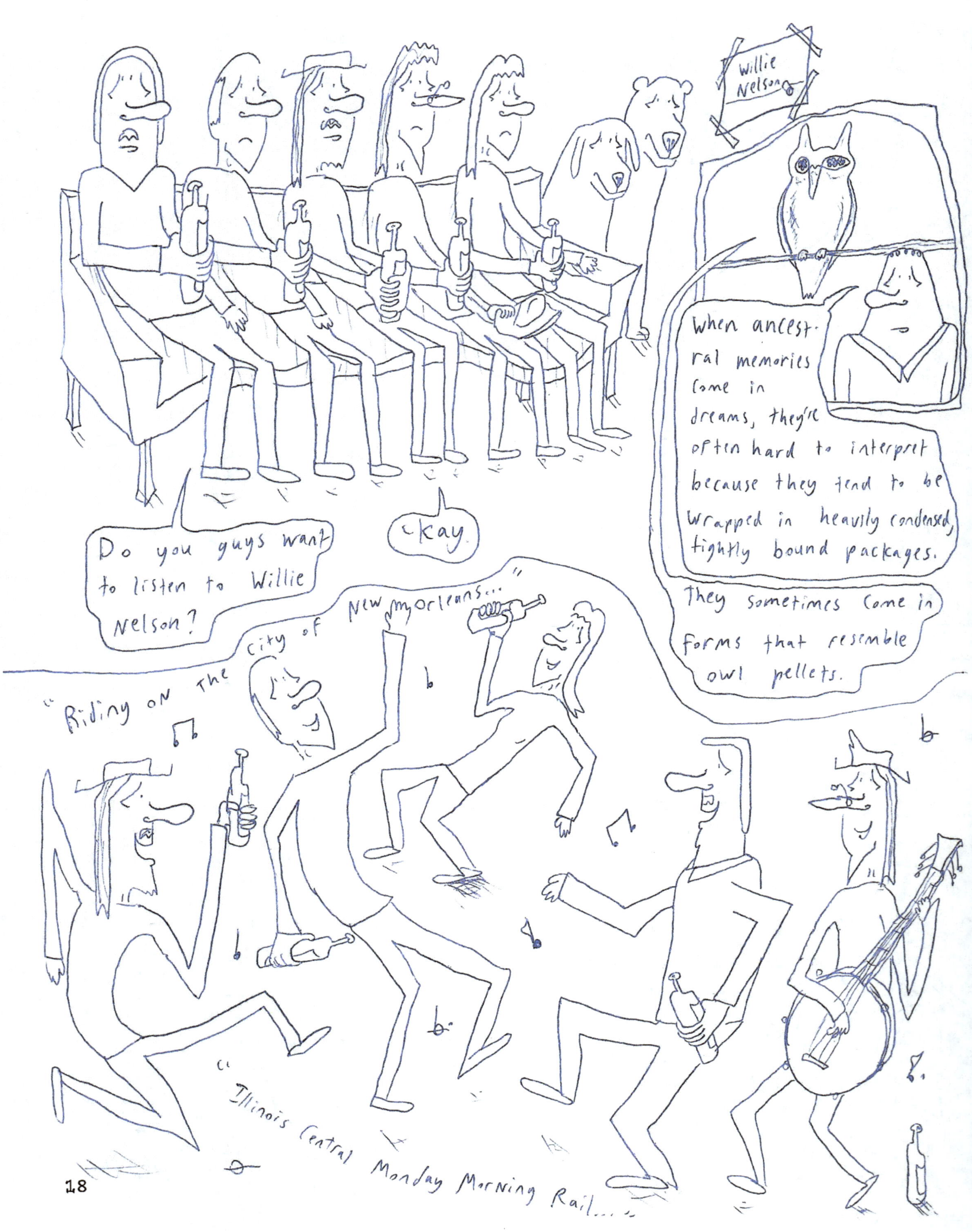

Willie Nelson
When ancestral memories come in dreams, they're often hard to interpret because they tend to be wrapped in heavily condensed, tightly bound packages.
They sometimes come in forms that resemble owl pellets.
Do you guys want to listen to Willie Nelson?
Okay.
"Riding on the city of New Orleans..."
Illinois Central Monday Morning Rail...

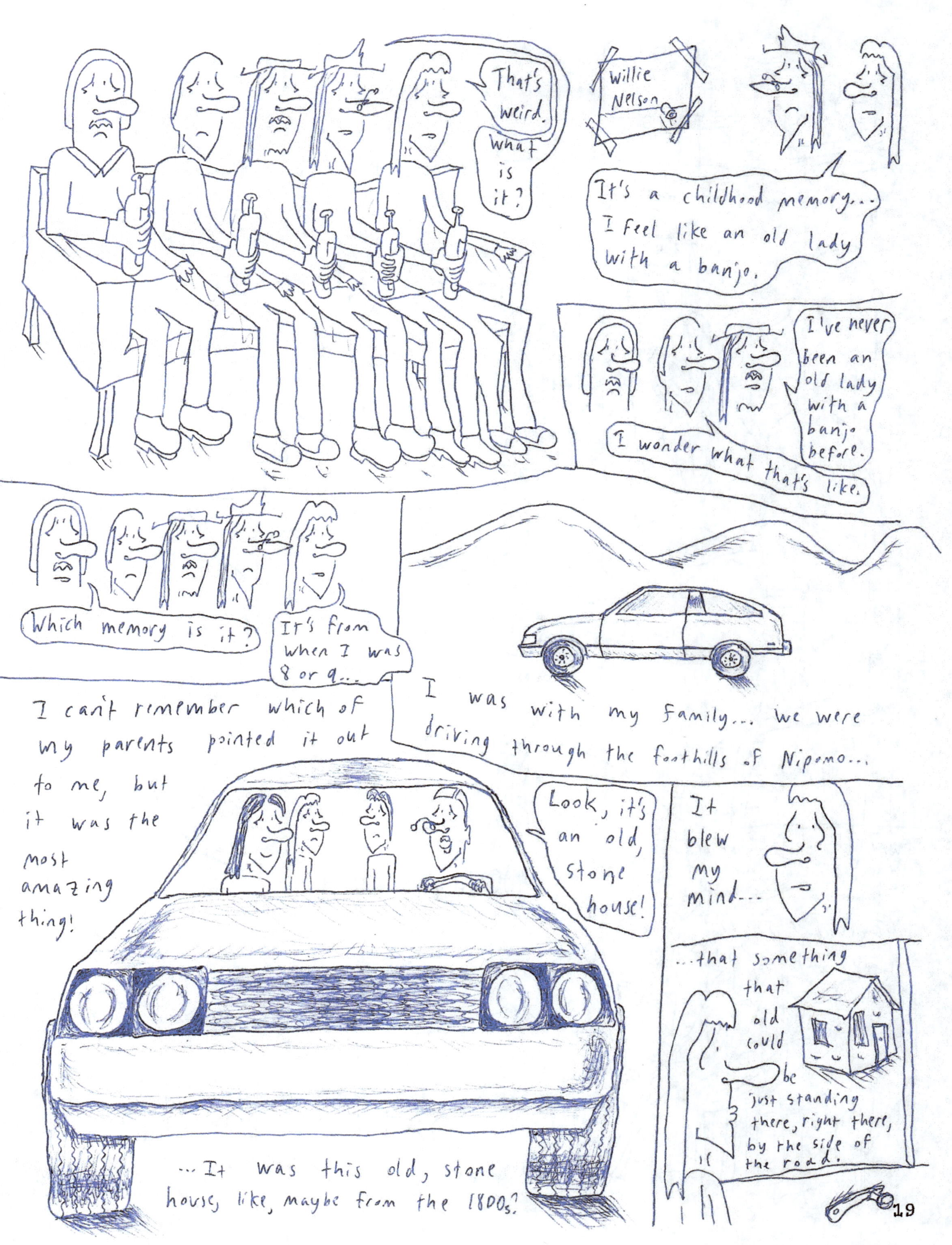

That's weird. What is it?
Willie Nelson
It's a childhood memory... I feel like an old lady with a banjo.
I've never been an old lady with a banjo before.
I wonder what that's like.
Which memory is it?
It's from when I was 8 or 9...
I can't remember which of my parents pointed it out to me, but it was the most amazing thing!
I was with my family... we were driving through the foothills of Nipomo...
Look, it's an old, stone house!
It blew my mind---
...that something that old could be just standing there, right there, by the side of the road!
...It was this old, stone house, like, maybe from the 1800s?

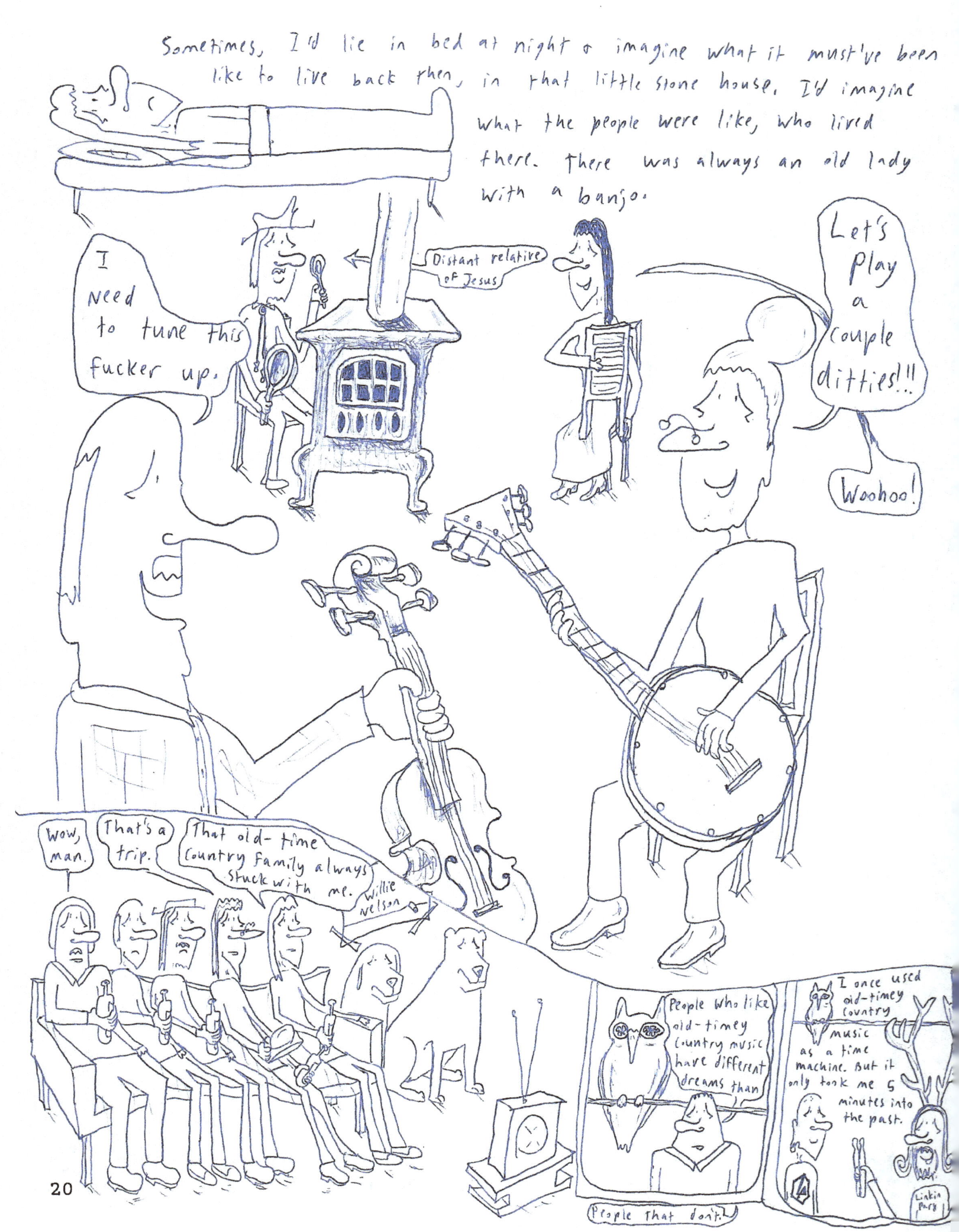

Sometimes, I'd lie in bed at night & imagine what it must've been like to live back then, in that little stone house. I'd imagine what the people were like, who lived there. There was always an old lady with a banjo.
I need to tune this fucker up.
Distant relative of Jesus
Let's play a couple ditties!!!
Woohoo!
Wow, man.
That's a trip.
That old-time country family always stuck with me.
Willie Nelson
People who like old-timey country music have different dreams than
People that don't.
I once used old-timey country music as a time machine. But it only took me 5 minutes into the past.
Linkin Park

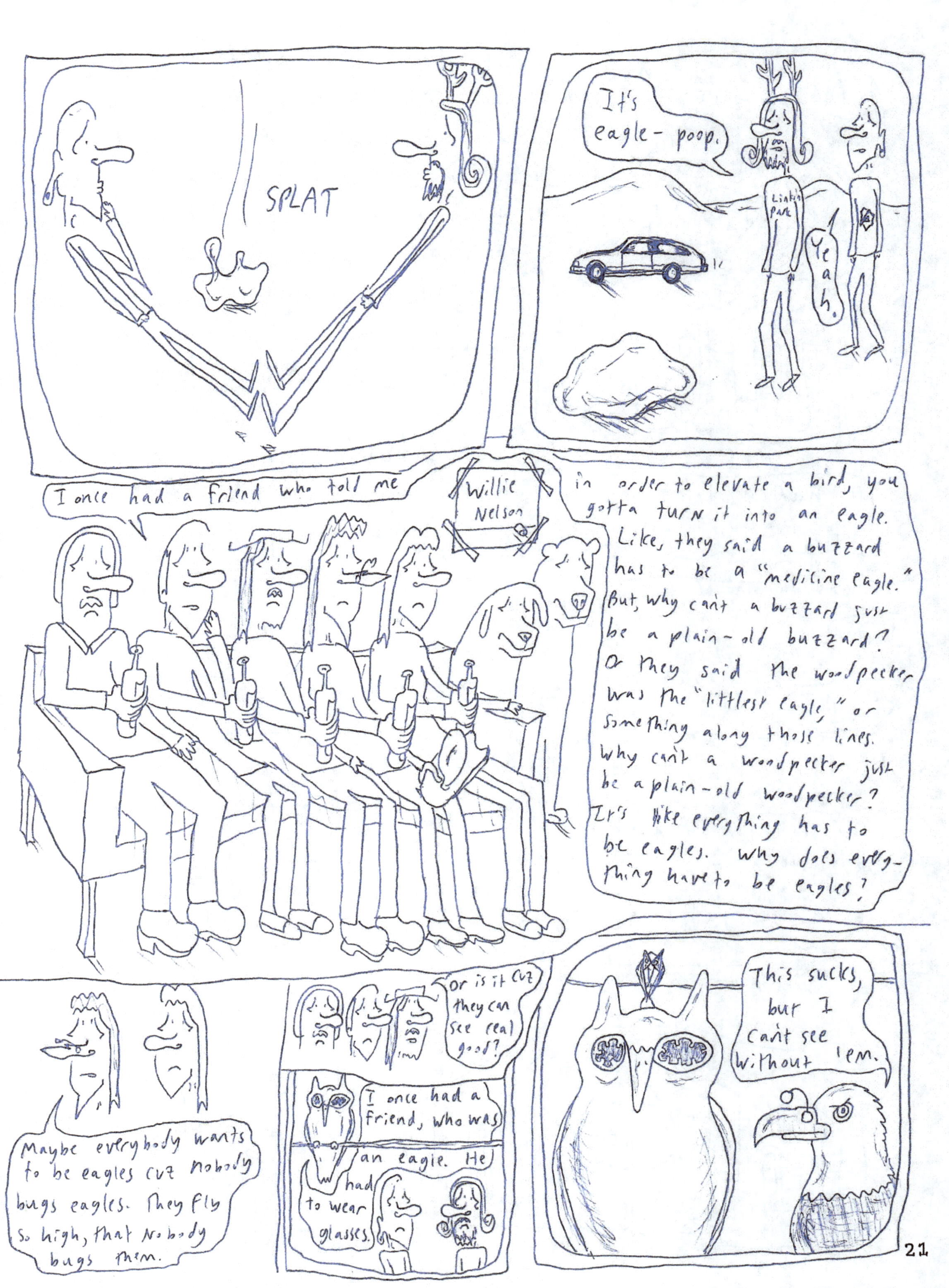
SPLAT

It's eagle-poop.

Linkin Park

Yeah.

I once had a friend who told me

Willie Nelson

in order to elevate a bird, you gotta turn it into an eagle. Like, they said a buzzard has to be a "medicine eagle." But, why can't a buzzard just be a plain-old buzzard? Or they said the woodpecker was the "littlest eagle," or something along those lines. Why can't a woodpecker just be a plain-old woodpecker? It's like everything has to be eagles. Why does everything have to be eagles?

Maybe everybody wants to be eagles cuz Nobody bugs eagles. They fly so high, that Nobody bugs them.

Or is it cuz they can see real good?

I once had a friend, who was an eagle. He had to wear glasses.

This sucks, but I can't see without 'em.

21

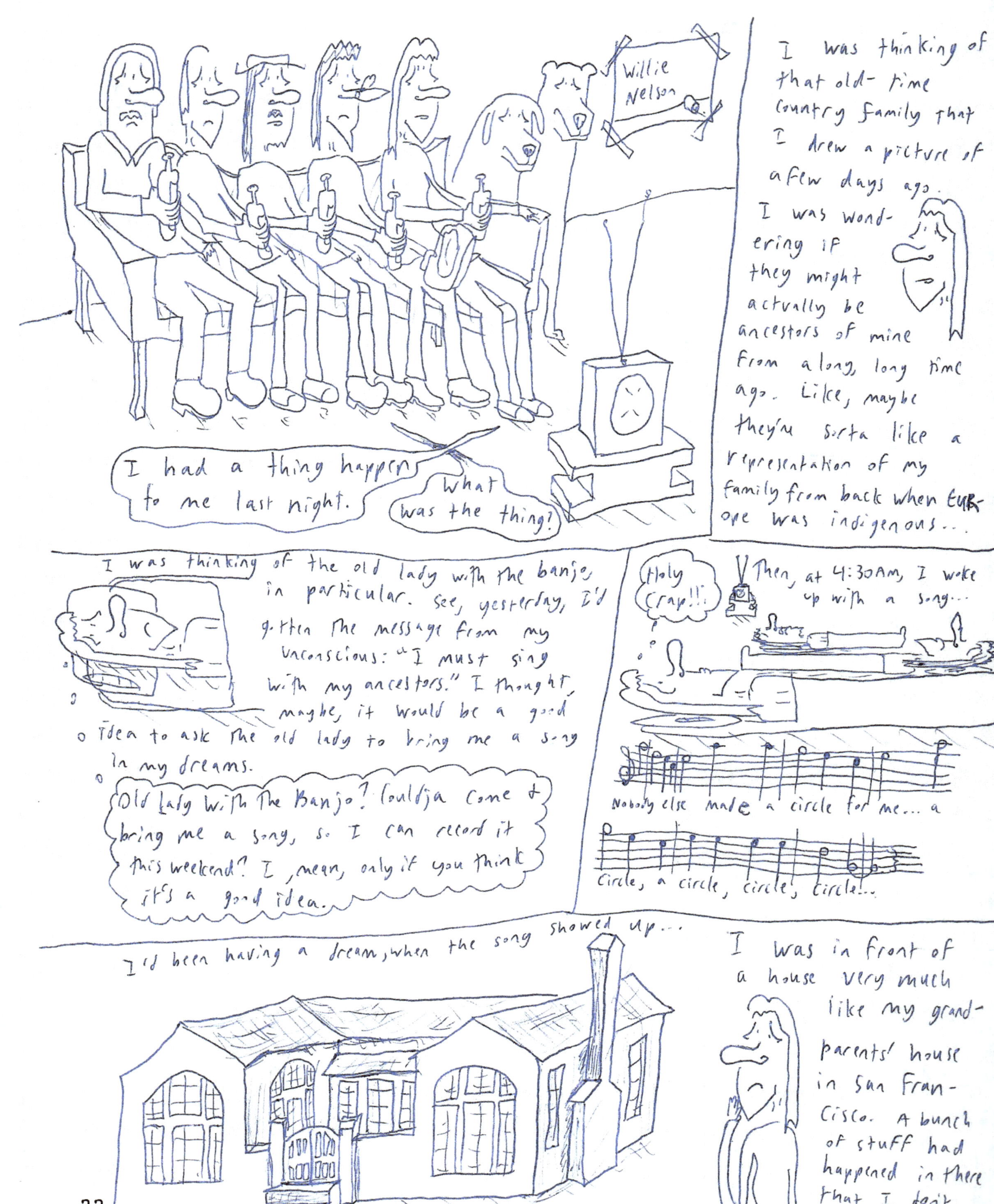

Willie Nelson
I had a thing happen to me last night.
What was the thing?
I was thinking of that old-time country family that I drew a picture of a few days ago. I was wondering if they might actually be ancestors of mine from a long, long time ago. Like, maybe they're sorta like a representation of my family from back when Europe was indigenous...
I was thinking of the old lady with the banjo, in particular. See, yesterday, I'd gotten the message from my unconscious: "I must sing with my ancestors." I thought, maybe, it would be a good idea to ask the old lady to bring me a song in my dreams.
Old lady with the Banjo! Couldja come & bring me a song, so I can record it this weekend? I, mean, only if you think it's a good idea.
Holy crap!!!
Then, at 4:30AM, I woke up with a song...
Nobody else made a circle for me... a circle, a circle, circle, circle...
I'd been having a dream, when the song showed up...
I was in front of a house very much like my grandparents' house in San Francisco. A bunch of stuff had happened in there that I don't remember too well...
22

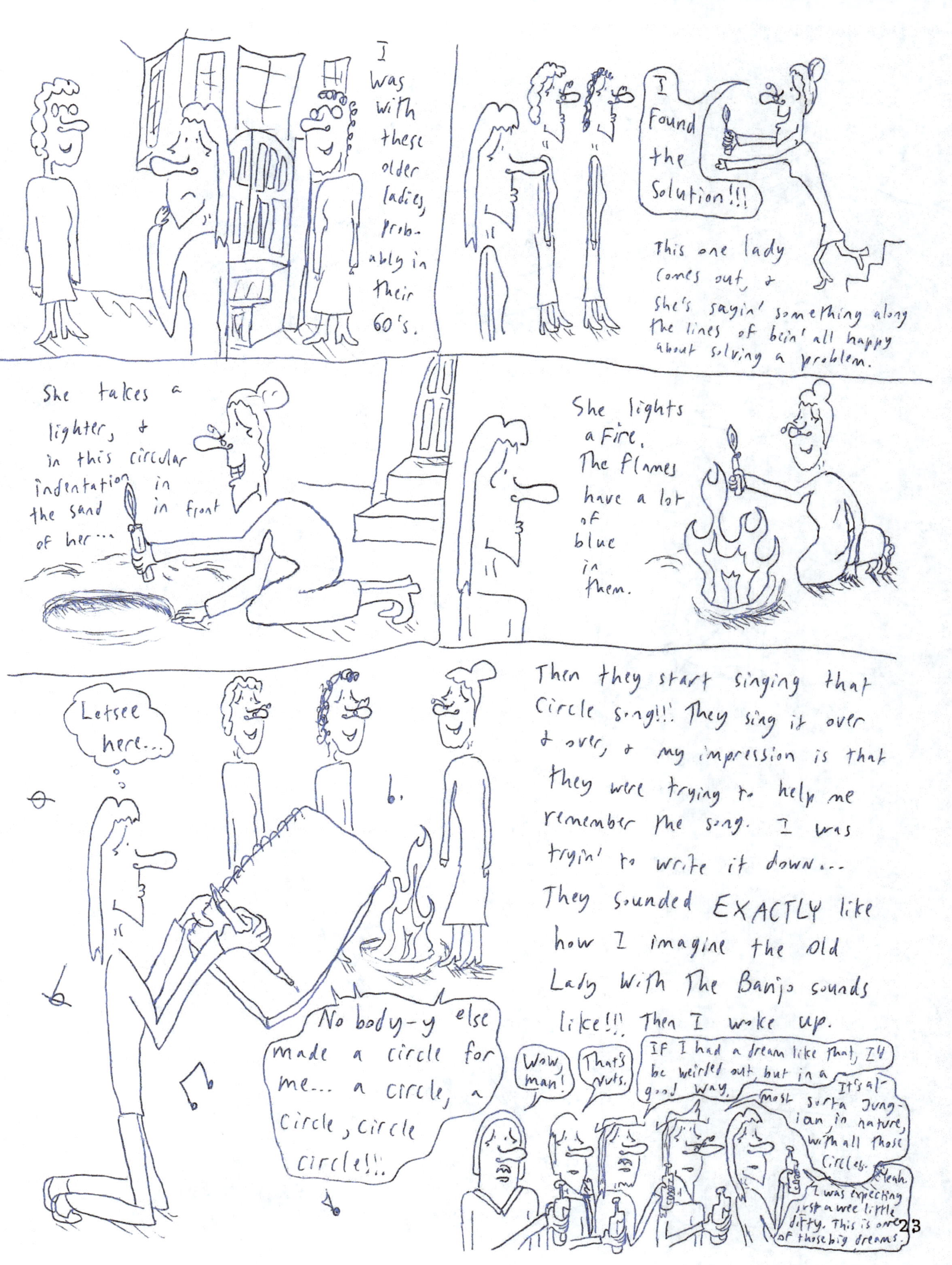

I was with these older ladies, prob- ably in their 60's.
I Found the Solution!!!
This one lady comes out, & she's sayin' something along the lines of bein' all happy about solving a problem.
She takes a lighter, & in this circular indentation in the sand in front of her...
She lights a Fire. The Flames have a lot of blue in them.
Letsee here...
No body-y else made a circle for me... a circle, a circle, circle circle circles!!
Then they start singing that Circle song!!! They sing it over & over, & my impression is that they were trying to help me remember the song. I was tryin' to write it down... They sounded EXACTLY like how I imagine the Old Lady With The Banjo sounds like!!! Then I woke up.
Wow man!
That's nuts.
If I had a dream like that, I'd be weirded out, but in a good way.
It's al- most sorta Jung- ian in nature, with all those circles.
Yeah. I was expecting just a wee little ditty. This is one of those big dreams.

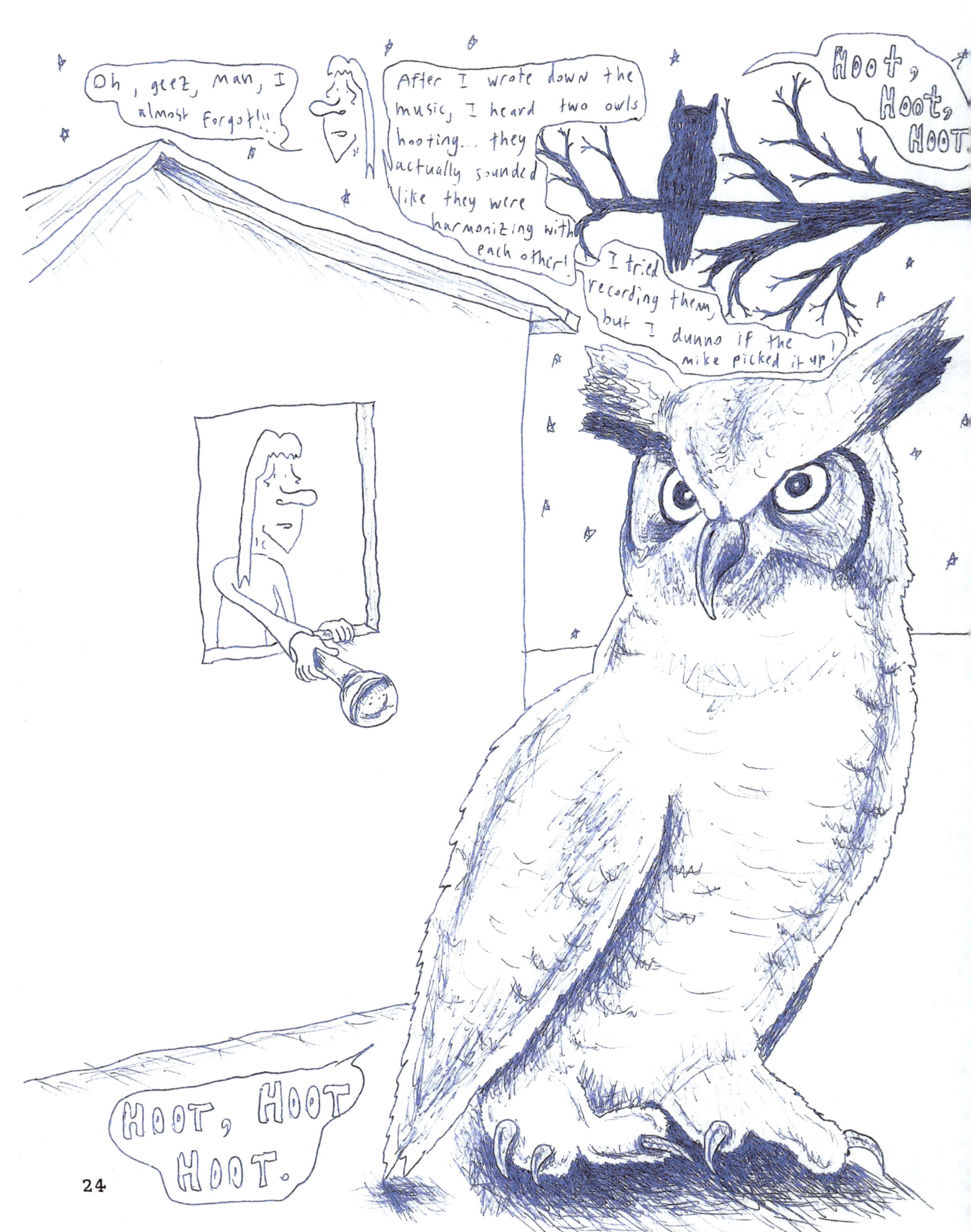

Oh, geez, man, I almost forgot!!!
After I wrote down the music, I heard two owls hooting... they actually sounded like they were harmonizing with each other!
I tried recording them, but I dunno if the mike picked it up!
Hoot, Hoot, Hoot
HOOT, HOOT HOOT.
24

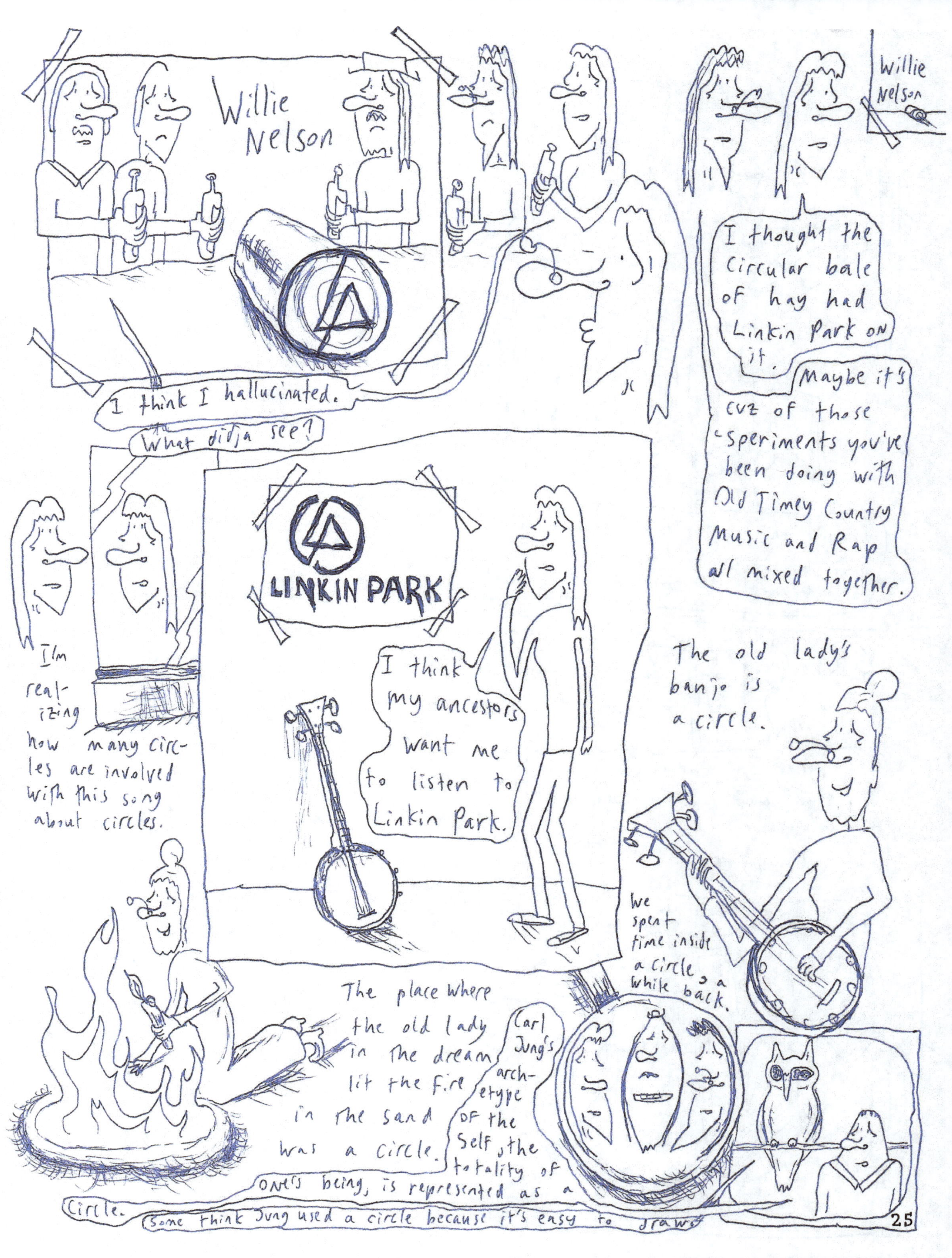

Willie Nelson
Willie Nelson
I think I hallucinated.
What didja see?
I thought the circular bale of hay had Linkin Park on it.
Maybe it's cuz of those 'speriments you've been doing with Old Timey Country Music and Rap all mixed together.
LINKIN PARK
I'm realizing how many circles are involved with this song about circles.
I think my ancestors want me to listen to Linkin Park.
The old lady's banjo is a circle.
We spent time inside a circle, a while back.
The place where the old lady in the dream lit the fire in the sand was a circle.
Carl Jung's archetype of the Self, the totality of one's being, is represented as a circle.
Some think Jung used a circle because it's easy to draw.

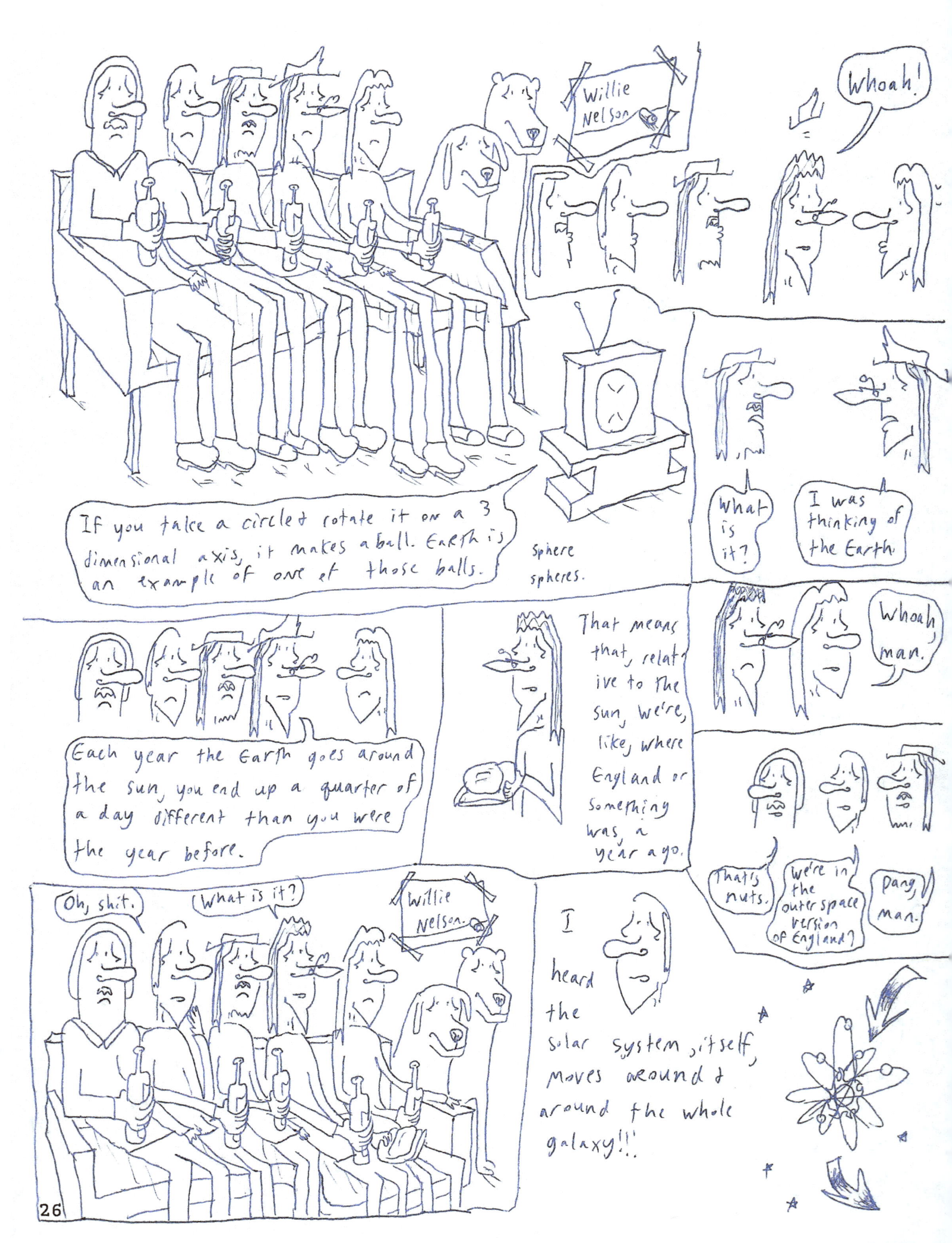

Willie Nelson
Whoah!
If you take a circle & rotate it on a 3 dimensional axis, it makes a ball. Earth is an example of one of those balls.
Sphere spheres.
What is it?
I was thinking of the Earth.
Each year the Earth goes around the sun, you end up a quarter of a day different than you were the year before.
That means that, relative to the sun, we're, like, where England or something was a year ago.
Whoah man.
That's nuts.
We're in the outer space version of England?
Dang, man.
Oh, shit.
What is it?
Willie Nelson.
I heard the solar system, itself, moves around & around the whole galaxy!!
26

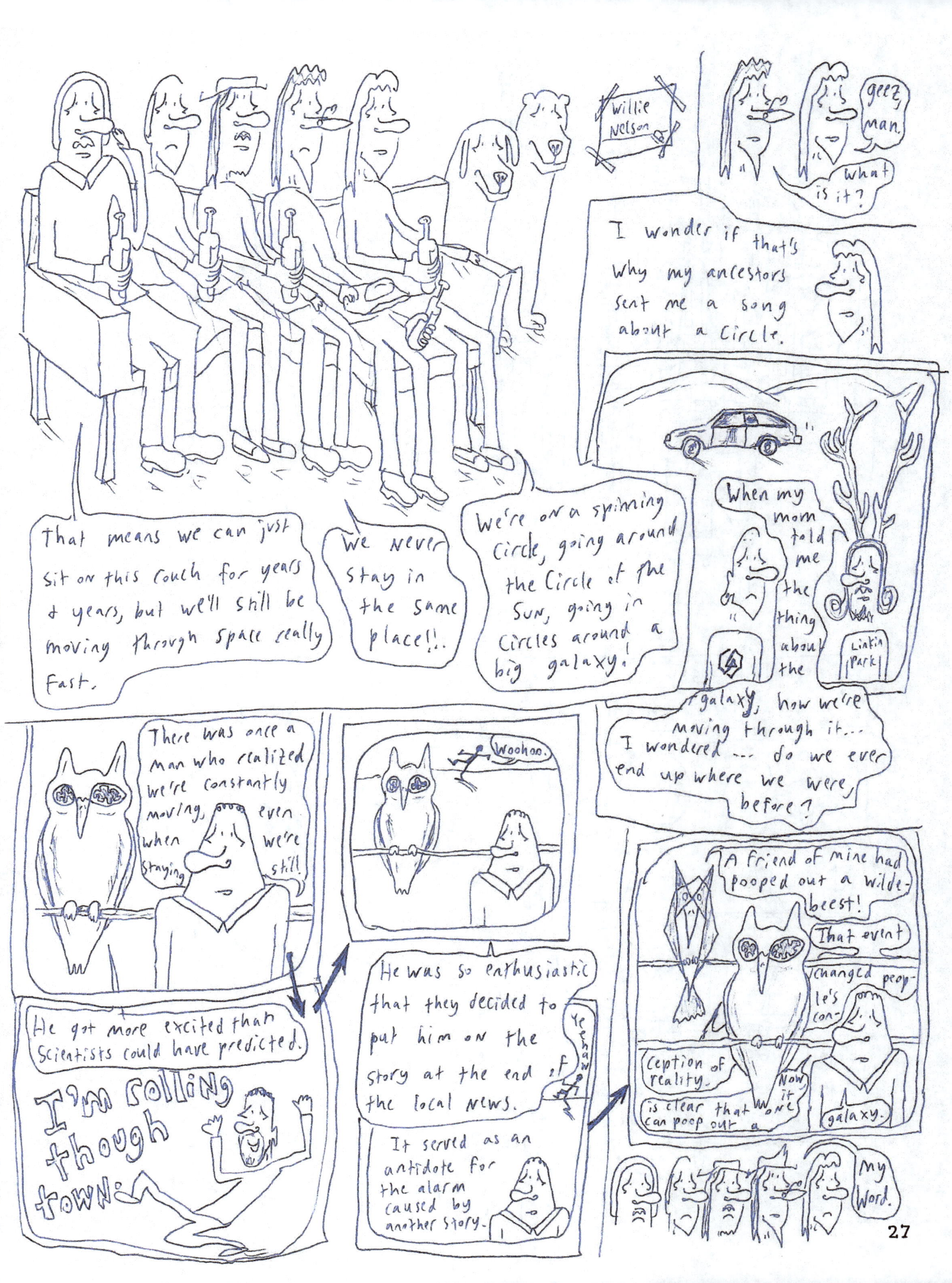

Willie Nelson
geez, man.
what is it?
I wonder if that's why my ancestors sent me a song about a circle.
That means we can just sit on this couch for years & years, but we'll still be moving through space really fast.
We never stay in the same place!!
We're on a spinning circle, going around the circle of the sun, going in circles around a big galaxy!
When my mom told me the thing about the galaxy, how we're moving through it... I wondered ... do we ever end up where we were, before?
Linkin Park
There was once a man who realized we're constantly moving, even when we're staying still.
Woohoo.
He got more excited than scientists could have predicted.
I'm rolling though town.
He was so enthusiastic that they decided to put him on the story at the end of the local news.
Yeehaw
It served as an antidote for the alarm caused by another story.
A friend of mine had pooped out a wildebeest!
That event changed people's conception of reality.
Now it is clear that no one can poop out a galaxy.
My word.

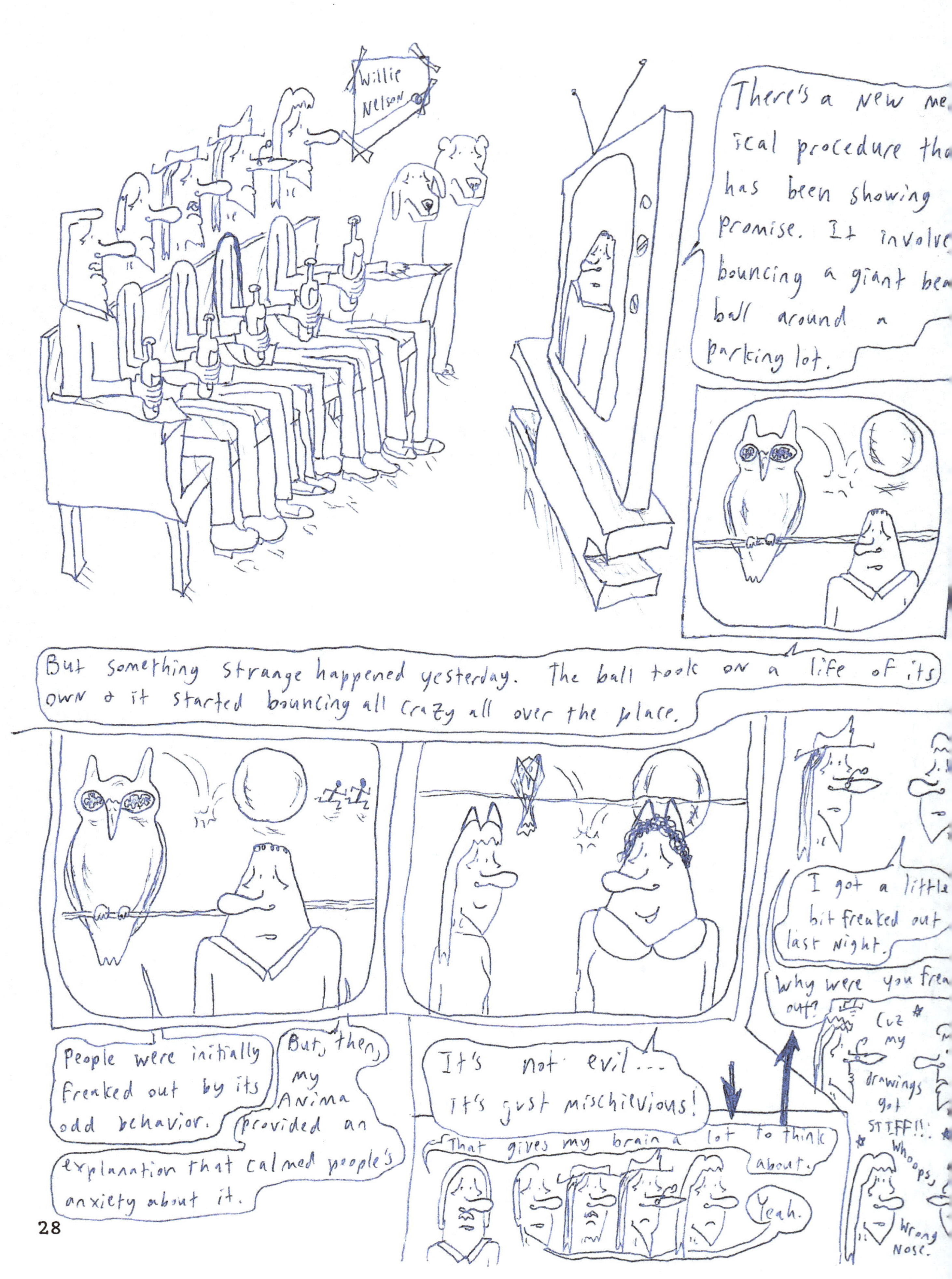

Willie Nelson
There's a new medical procedure that has been showing promise. It involves bouncing a giant beach ball around a parking lot.
But something strange happened yesterday. The ball took on a life of its own & it started bouncing all crazy all over the place.
People were initially freaked out by its odd behavior.
But, then, my Anima provided an explanation that calmed people's anxiety about it.
It's not evil... It's just mischievous!
That gives my brain a lot to think about.
Yeah.
I got a little bit freaked out last night.
Why were you freaked out?
Cuz my drawings got STIFF!!
Whoops, wrong nose.

28

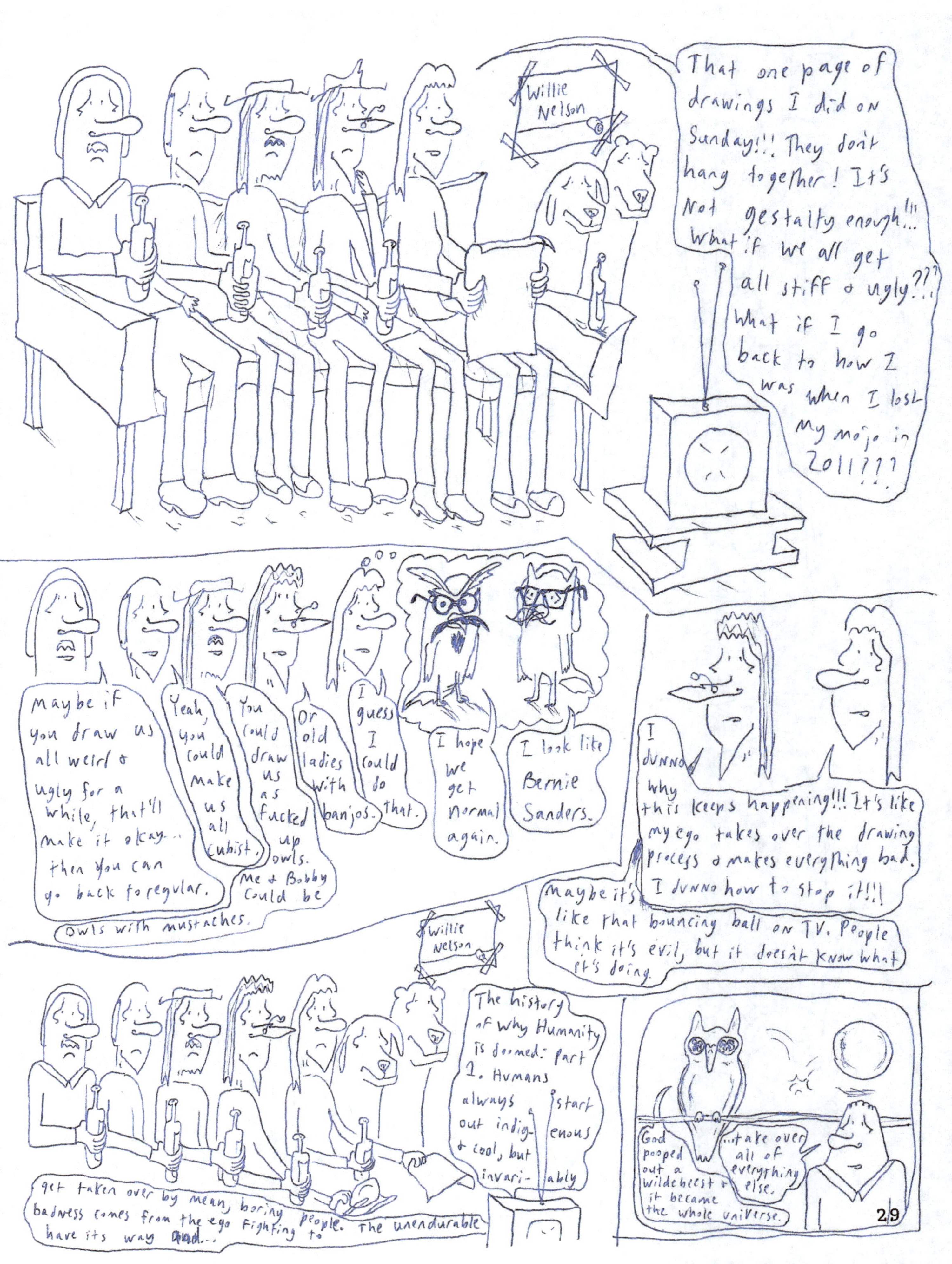

Willie Nelson
That one page of drawings I did on Sunday!!! They don't hang together! It's Not gestalty enough!!! What if we all get all stiff & ugly??? What if I go back to how I was when I lost My mojo in 2011???
Maybe if you draw us all weird & ugly for a while, that'll make it okay... then you can go back to regular.
Yeah, you could make us all cubist.
You could draw us as fucked up owls. Me & Bobby could be
Or old ladies with banjos.
I guess I could do that.
I hope we get normal again.
I look like Bernie Sanders.
Owls with mustaches.
I dunno why this keeps happening!!! It's like my ego takes over the drawing process & makes everything bad. I dunno how to stop it!!!
maybe it's like that bouncing ball on TV. People think it's evil, but it doesn't know what it's doing.
Willie Nelson
The history of why Humanity is doomed: part 1. Humans always start out indigenous & cool, but invari-ably get taken over by mean, boring people. The unendurable badness comes from the ego Fighting to have its way...
God pooped out a wildebeest & it became the whole universe.
...take over all of everything else.
29

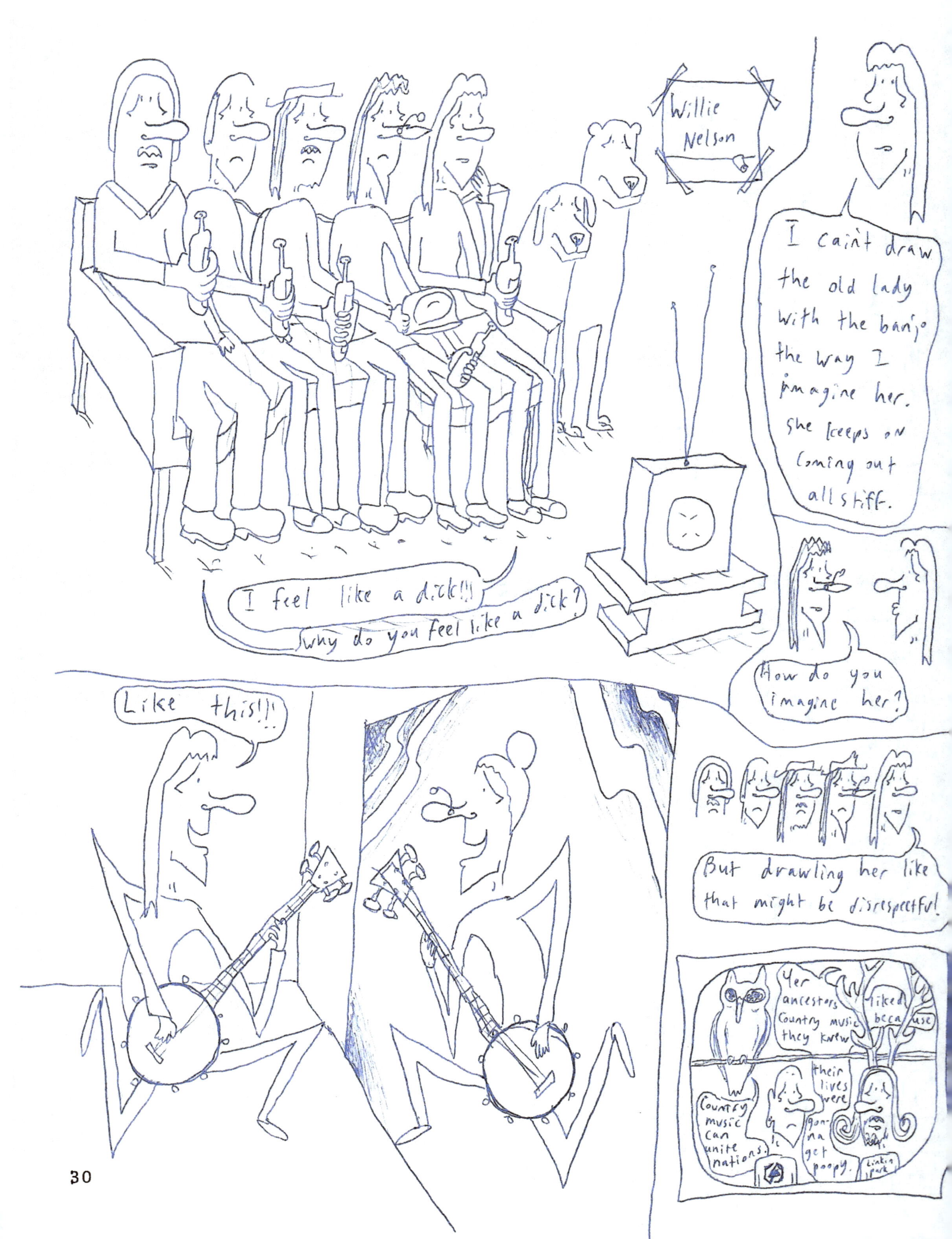

Willie Nelson
I cain't draw the old lady with the banjo the way I imagine her. She keeps on coming out all stiff.
I feel like a dick!!!
Why do you feel like a dick?
How do you imagine her?
Like this!!!
But drawing her like that might be disrespectful!
Yer ancestors liked country music because they knew their lives were gonna get poopy.
Country music can unite nations.
Linkin Park

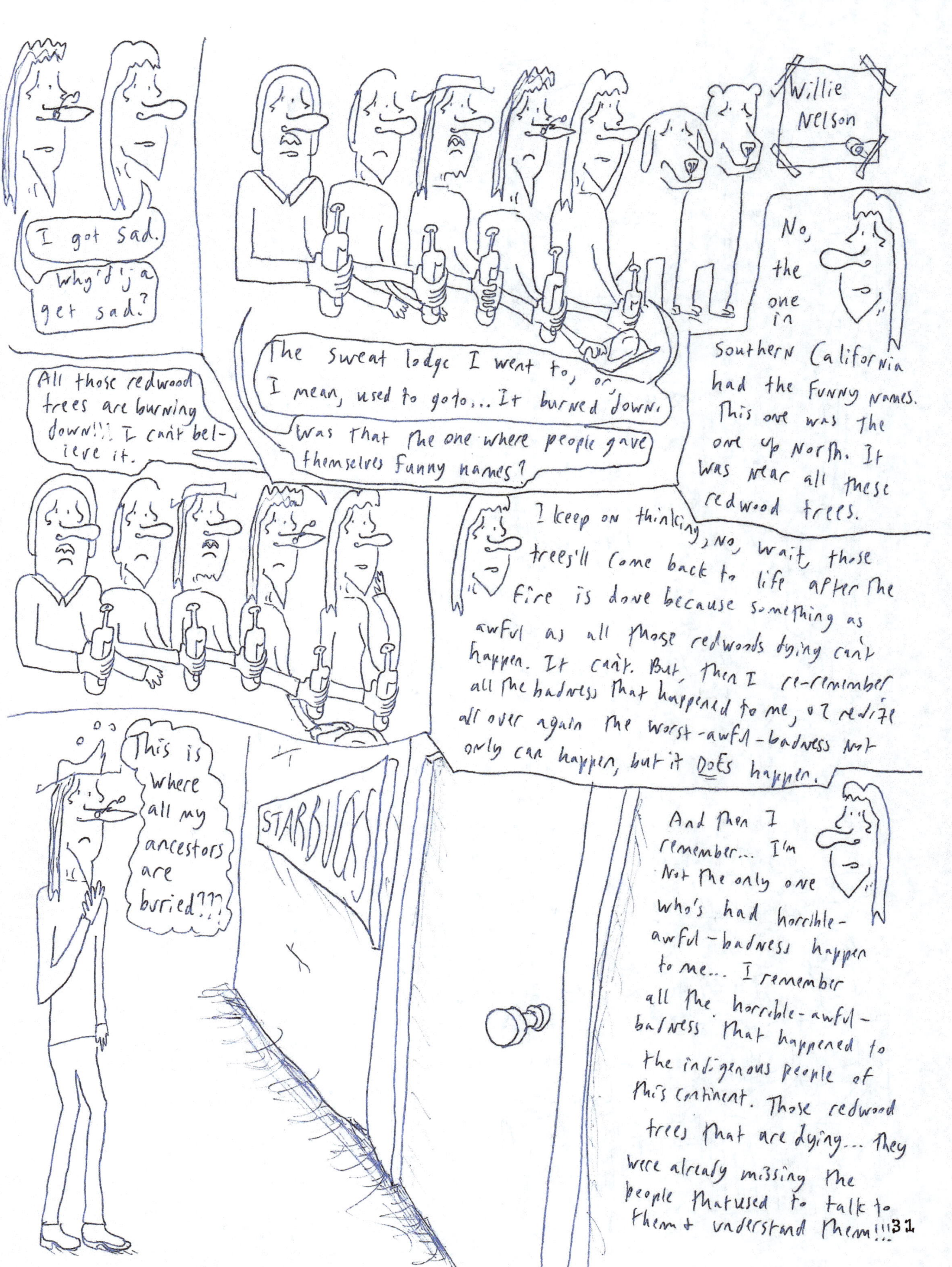

I got sad.
Why'dija get sad?
All those redwood trees are burning down!!! I can't believe it.
The sweat lodge I went to, or I mean, used to go to... It burned down. Was that the one where people gave themselves funny names?
Willie Nelson
No, the one in Southern California had the funny names. This one was the one up North. It was near all these redwood trees.
I keep on thinking, No, wait, those trees'll come back to life after the fire is done because something as awful as all those redwoods dying can't happen. It can't. But, then I re-remember all the badness that happened to me, or realize all over again the worst-awful-badness not only can happen, but it DOES happen.
This is where all my ancestors are buried!!!
STARBUCKS
And then I remember... I'm not the only one who's had horrible-awful-badness happen to me... I remember all the horrible-awful-badness that happened to the indigenous people of this continent. Those redwood trees that are dying... They were already missing the people that used to talk to them & understand them!!!

31

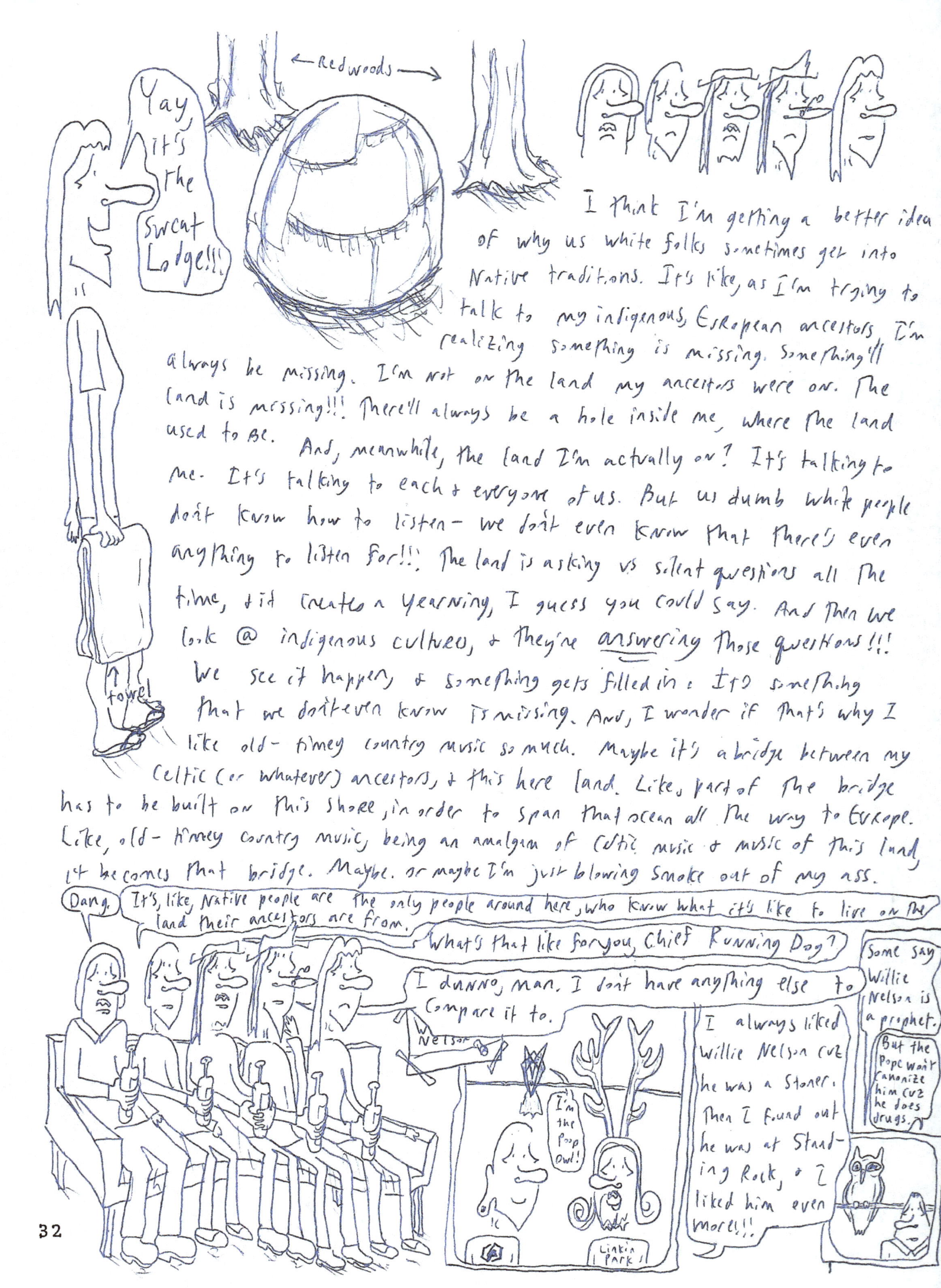

I think I'm getting a better idea of why us white folks sometimes get into Native traditions. It's like, as I'm trying to talk to my indigenous, European ancestors, I'm realizing something is missing. Something'll always be missing. I'm not on the land my ancestors were on. The land is missing!!! There'll always be a hole inside me, where the land used to be. And, meanwhile, the land I'm actually on? It's talking to me. It's talking to each & everyone of us. But us dumb white people don't know how to listen — we don't even know that there's even anything to listen for!!! The land is asking us silent questions all the time, & it creates a yearning, I guess you could say. And then we look @ indigenous cultures, & they're <u>answering</u> those questions!!! We see it happen, & something gets filled in. It's something that we don't even know is missing. And, I wonder if that's why I like old-timey country music so much. Maybe it's a bridge between my Celtic (or whatever) ancestors, & this here land. Like, part of the bridge has to be built on this shore, in order to span that ocean all the way to Europe. Like, old-timey country music, being an amalgam of Celtic music & music of this land, it becomes that bridge. Maybe. or maybe I'm just blowing smoke out of my ass.

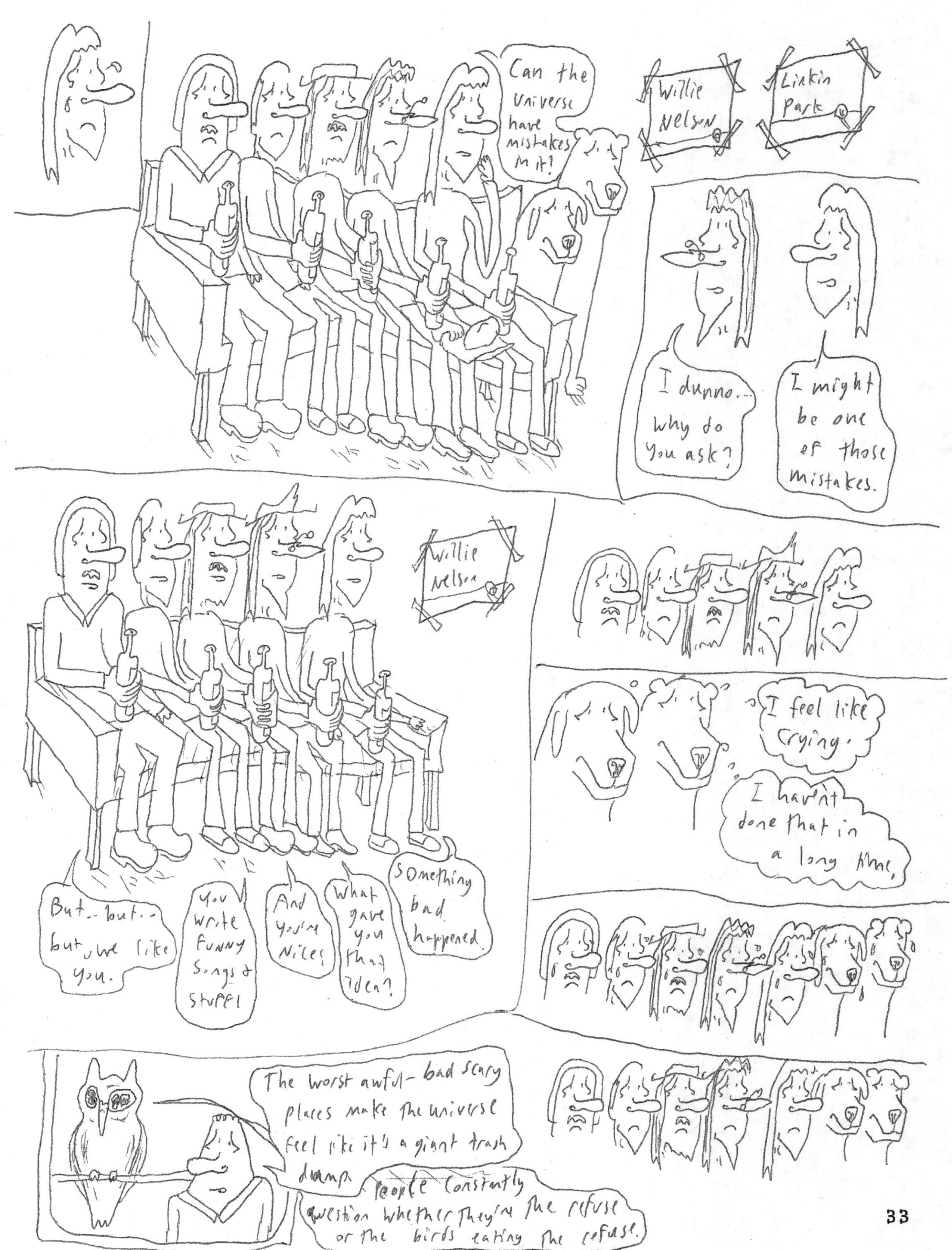

Can the universe have mistakes in it?
Willie Nelson
Linkin Park
I dunno... why do you ask?
I might be one of those mistakes.
Willie Nelson
I feel like crying.
I haven't done that in a long time.
But--but-- but we like you.
You write funny songs & stuff!
And you're nice!
What gave you that idea?
Something bad happened
The worst awful--bad scary places make the universe feel like it's a giant trash dump. People constantly question whether they're the refuse or the birds eating the refuse.

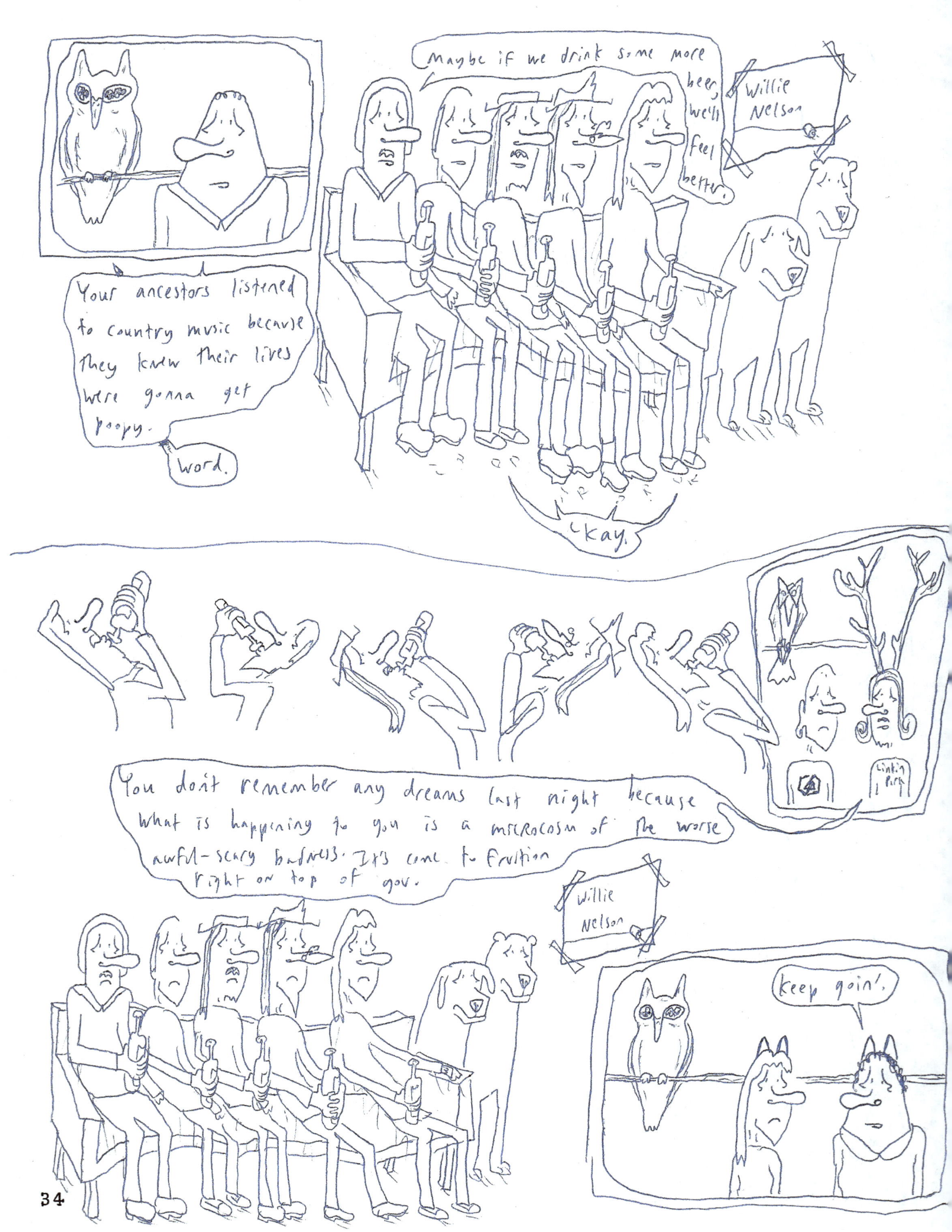

Maybe if we drink some more beer, we'll feel better.
Willie Nelson
okay.
Your ancestors listened to country music because they knew their lives were gonna get poopy.
word.
You don't remember any dreams last night because what is happening to you is a microcosm of the worse awful-scary badness. It's come to fruition right on top of you.
Linkin Park
Willie Nelson
keep goin'.

Notes

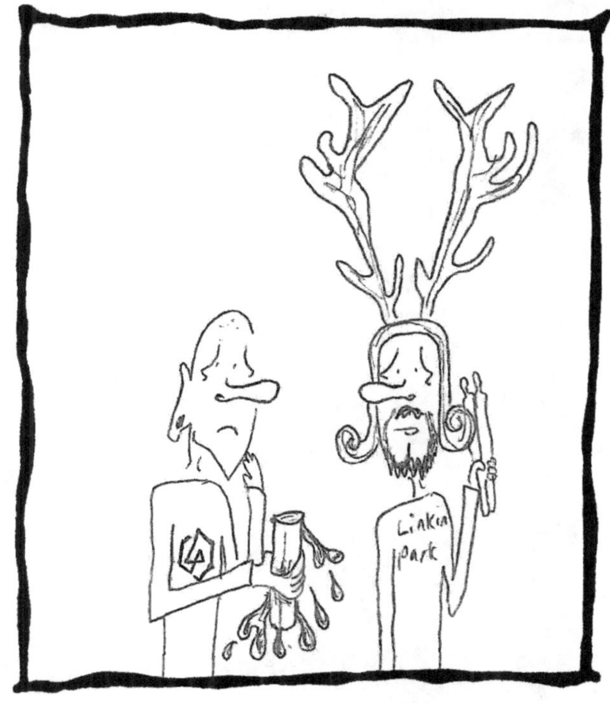

Introduction: For more on the topic of active imagination, see: Johnson, R. A. (1991). *Owning Your Own Shadow: Understanding the Dark Side of the Psyche*. New York: HarperCollins.

Page 1: You get to see more about the energy that's stuck to me on page 2.

 Music ghosts are discussed in Part 4 of the *Hell* series. They can be ghosts who make music, or they can be the ghosts of music. There's also the idea that every song has a ghost in it, or infinite ghosts, I should say. These particular music ghosts are what you end up with if you carve certain frequencies out of songs. You take that old harmonic series, and you can come up with all sorts of new songs that exist within the signal coming from a tape recorder.

The owl is also referring to how I used to be a silly kid, who did silly stuff on tape recorders. Life came along and took some of that silliness away from me; I hope I can reclaim it at some point.

The History of Sadness – while not having had that title at the time – was addressed in Part 3 – in that book, I came to terms with the horrible things that can happen (and do happen) to people. I made the realization that none of us are safe – not a single, solitary, blessed soul. Horrible, awful badness can happen to everyone, as I discovered through my horrible health condition. That's part of what the History of Sadness refers to – the History of Sadness is just plain old sadness, but it's also horrible, awful, bad things.

The black guy on the TV is referring to a trial by fire – little did I know I was about a month away from, yet, another trial by fire (geez, man – one horrible thing a year is enough – now there's a second horrible thing I'm going through – but at least I can deal with this second one, as much as it sucks). The thing about the smoke god – that became the theme of the next album I'm working on.

Page 2: I think the thing about being a kid and hot dogs, and all that, is pretty self-explanatory. I still don't understand why those adults made such a big deal about me not wanting condiments. Like – really? Who gives a fuck????

What the black guy and the owl are talking about is something I think about a lot. How much of me is me, and how much of what I think of as me is actually energy that doesn't belong to me?

The words, "the shape of your soul is correct" came spontaneously. I hope that owl is right about that. He might be speaking to how my soul is just fine, but my incarnation in this life is not fine, despite my soul being fine. This incarnation did not turn out fine because I have all that energy that doesn't belong to me bollixing things up – it's like a ghost in the machine or something.

Page 3: The owls in the window played big roles in previous *Hell* books.

Relaxed control – I could use some of that – I'm not sure, all-the-way, what it is, but it sounds good for someone like me, who has Generalized Anxiety Disorder. The cans of it bleeding because the land was stolen from the indigenous people of this land – that makes me wonder. Maybe the whole of this land is bleeding because of that theft. I wouldn't be surprised if the land was bleeding – along similar lines, I think the spirits of the land are crying – they cry all the time.

Page 4: I remember when my first car was dying, its spirit literally left. The reason I know that is the feeling of the car had changed – it felt like it was black inside. When I was about to trade it in for another car, suddenly the car felt the way it had before – its spirit came back. I recognized that old feeling, and I knew the car was saying goodbye to me. The car's spirit came back to say goodbye. That was the day I realized cars have souls.

There are places I've walked around that have that same, strange, empty feeling to them. Like, there're certain parts of Santa Clara, CA, for example that feel that way. It always makes me wonder if an atrocity was committed in that area, and that made the soul of the land leave.

The day I did this page, I was looking at a doorknob, and I tripped out. It was a shiny surface, and I realized the only thing I could see was gold colored reflections of the room I was in. That tripped me out – it wasn't just this separate object I was seeing (a doorknob) – I was seeing a distorted, round version of the room I was in.

Page 5: I start to work on looking at ancestral trauma here – I had ancestors in the 1906 earthquake in San Francisco. As you'll see later on, the ancestral work goes back even farther than this. It's something I'm continuing to work on.

I was blown away when the owl said music is a soul. It makes sense on an intuitive level for me – and at the same time, it trips me out.

Page 6: My relationship to the color yellow has changed a lot over the course of my life. For some reason, when I was a kid, I didn't like the color yellow – but these days, yellow looks like such a happy color to me. When I imagine the color yellow, I see all these prismatic rainbows in it. Maybe I should do a painting of that, now that I think of it. But, when I was a kid, yellow was problematic for me – I had an aversion to yellow food, in particular (except maybe stuff made from lemons).

It trips me out that the extent of what the human eye can see is just the visible spectrum, which is just a teeny tiny bit of the entire spectrum of light. I can't even imagine colors outside of the visible spectrum – and, yet, I hear insects and stuff can see some of those other frequencies of light. Like, what? How can there be other colors? How? The black guy and the owl talk about how the visible spectrum looks complete – it makes a circle. How could there be other colors, if what we see forms a gestalt, a circle? How???

Page 7: Dang, I remember that yellow tumbler in the bathroom from when I was a kid. There was a blue one, a pink one, and a yellow one. I never wanted to drink outta the yellow one.

I still hate mustard – that's something I hate, to this day. I like other yellow types of food now, though. Eggs are fine. But mustard? That's one I could never learn to like.

Yeah, that's a real childhood memory. I don't know how tall the plate of scrambled eggs was in real life, but as a little kid, it looked gargantuan. I should ask my brother if he remembers how big the plate of eggs was. I'm not even sure what we were doing in the neighbor lady's kitchen that day.

I once wrote a vampire story, and "sun shadowing" was when vampires go out into the sun and turn to dust. It's the vampire version of suicide. I'd never thought of ghosts as hiding in the sun, but if there are sun-ghosts, that would be an ideal place to hide. It's like they're hidden in plain sight because everyone'll go blind if they look at them for too long.

Antique furniture with ghosts in it: There was this antique dresser thingy my parents bought when I was a kid. It had a ghost in it. Both me and my sister-in-law sensed it. As soon as my parents sold the dresser thingy, the bedroom it was in (the bedroom I slept in) felt a lot less ghosty.

Page 8: I was feeling really low self esteem-y that day, and I was pretty sure the people I was staying with were getting tired of me. It gave me that black, spirit-less feeling.

Back in 2011, when I first started doing Jesus and Chief Running Dog books, I hit a rough patch, where I suddenly couldn't draw Chief Running Dog anymore. All the drawings came out really ugly, and as the me-character implies – there was no soul in the drawings. I tried to replicate the ugly drawings on this page, but these drawings aren't nearly as ugly as the ones I did in 2011.

Page 9: I thought I might have had covid-19, so I went and got a test. See, I was staying with some people (the very people who might've been getting tired of me), and I was afraid I was gonna give it to them – so I got a test to make sure I didn't have it. I didn't. But, it was odd – the testing place was at this park, and there really were crows there – corvids at the covid testing. I usually like watching crows because they're such neat looking birds, but that day, I didn't feel in the mood. That was probably cuz I was having anxiety.

That was a real dream I had that morning.

Page 10: I was just about to say, "I'm not sure who the reinforcements are that the antler guy is talking about," but now that I'm thinking of it, I do know – at least I know who mine would be. There's stuff later on about a lost twin. That's probably who my reinforcement is.

When I was a baby, I remember having an out-of-body experience, during which I talked to one of my spirit guides. I was a very unhappy baby, but this was a happy babyhood memory – I remember bein' really happy and at peace, floating around, talking to this spirit guide. I always wonder if, when I gained the ability to speak, if I lost the ability to talk to my spirit-friends. In other words, I wonder if I lost my native language when I learned to speak, because that language got displaced by English. Along similar lines, I feel like I've never quite fit in with this world; in learning to be in it – and sucking at it – did I lose my natural way of being? I'm guessing lots of people feel that way.

I remember when Charlie and Daisy, my kitties, were still alive, I thought of shmoos. Are shmoos cat-shaped ghosts? Or are they the ghosts of cats?

Page 11: My apologies to Lester Holt – I hope the pictures of him don't look too caricature-ish. I love Lester Holt – he's such a great news caster. He just seems to have such a gentle way about him. The stuff about the left and right side of the body being impacted differently by covid is made up, but my health condition affects the right side worse than the left side. Oddly enough, it seems like my right side is negatively impacted by all kinds of things. For example, my right eye is my bad eye, and I get menstrual cramps mainly on the right side.

Page 12: I was thinking of the idea that I have a lost twin – like, another soul that shoulda been a twin of me in this life. But I hadn't considered the possibility that *I* was the lost twin! My, my, my.

The story of the two trees is true – that happened back in – hmm – 2014? Maybe. Or maybe it was 2015 – I'm not sure.

Page 13: Yeah, as counter-intuitive as that old spirit name was – given the fact there's only one of me – I knew it was the real deal. Or at least, I think I knew it was the real deal. That later discovery of the 2-ness of all my characters cemented the whole thing for me.

There was a place that sold paint when I was a little kid that had my favorite commercial song – the San Luis Paint Factory. The song I heard in the sweat lodge wasn't that song, *per se*, but it was the same style. It'd be cool if my cosmic twin really did send me that song. I hope me and her get reunited some day.

Page 14: That was a true story – the night after doin' all this writing about lost twins – there was that story on Gray's Anatomy – these 2 twins were attached at the head.

I'm SO slow on the uptake. There was a little bit of space at the bottom of the page, and I was all, what should I put there? I'm not sure what gave me the idea of putting a burrowing owl there – it seemed totally random at the time. It wasn't till weeks later that I looked at the picture and went, duh. I spent all this time talking about holes – and burrowing owls make holes.

I actually do have the feeling of there being a hole in my right side. It's been there for years. I'd never thought about it as being where me and my cosmic twin were supposed to be joined – but that would satisfyingly explain why the dang thing never heals or gets filled in.

I'm not sure, all-the-way, what the football helmet signifies, but I think it has a lot to do with how horrible our culture is and how we're divorced from the natural way we should be. I'm guessing the football helmet probably represents the ways we try to fill in the gaps we have in our psyches, due to losing our indigenous ways.

Page 15: Okay, that was real – that shamanic healing workshop-thing, where I got felt up. I feel kinda bad about bein' snarky about that one woman's experience where she set free all those Native folks stuck in limbo. Who knows? Maybe she really did. I feel like a butt for bein' snarky, but then again, I'm just reporting my experience.

Page 16: Okay, wow, this page is the launching point of some of the ancestral exploration I do in this book. I was in the shower when the idear of not having a bridge to my once-indigenous ancestors came to me. I used sofa cushions as the image for a makeshift bridge cuz it's one of those little kid-ish images. Like, you know how kids make forts outta sofa cushions? It's like that. Like, none of us seem equipped to connect with our indigenous ancestors – we're all winging it. We're as effective as a dude using couch cushions to do it.

Page 17: Sometimes depression feels like a cardboard box to me. I'm not sure how to describe it. It's like, well, dry – like cardboard. And it's the color of cardboard. And you feel stuck in it, as if you're in a box.

 As you can tell by now, I've been into indigenous spirituality for some time. But I started to feel conflicted about it in recent years because of the whole cultural appropriation piece. It's so terrible that us white folks and the US government and all made it illegal for indigenous folks to practice their spirituality. And then we come along and say, wait, I want a piece of that. That's really obnoxious.

 As I mention on this page, it makes sense we'd be drawn to it, since living on this land has a huge impact on us – those practices are so entwined with this land that they would logically feel natural to us. This is something I grapple with a lot. I don't want to be a culturally appropriating dick, so I stopped engaging in Native practices; and at the same time, I'm all sad cuz I miss it – those practices resonate with me a lot.

Page 18: This is where we start to look at how country music is so intimately tied in with my ancestral memories. You'll see more on that in a bit. It's odd – there's something about country music that I have a deep connection to – there's something about it that speaks to my soul – it's as if it's the language of my soul.

I love Willie Nelson – there's something really pure and nice about his music. And City of New Orleans is a great song.

Page 19: That's a real childhood memory. I tried to faithfully reproduce the car my parents had when I was a kid – it was a Toyota Celica – I believe from 1979.

I don't know how old that old stone house was in real life. For all I know it was just some shed on someone's yard. But I saw it as bein' from the 1800s, which in California, is old. Not in Europe, though.

Page 20: That country family has stuck with me through the years. There were a couple recent times I recorded songs that reminded me of how I imagine that old lady with a banjo as sounding. In making this book, I realized the possibility that that family might represent my indigenous European ancestors.

Page 21: I felt compelled to put the Toyota Celica in the frame with the 2 guys. It's almost like a dream image, a dreamed-up image of a memory that's always with me. I hear that the unconscious is timeless – it exists in all times. Similarly, the car exists in all times. It's this weird, Dali-esque dream-thingy.

No offense to people who compare other birds to eagles. No, it's more like, it's my (and Timmy's) preference to call birds by their actual names. But if other people wanna call them some kind of eagle, it's all good. The idea of an eagle wearing glasses came spontaneously. It made me laugh.

Page 22: Okay, wow, yeah – this was real. It happened to me.

Page 23: I couldn't believe it when I woke up hearing that song in my head! It sounded exactly like how I imagine the old lady with the banjo as sounding – both the style of the music, and the way the vocals sounded! I really feel like my ancestors were speaking to me that night. The song is posted on beckyshomemadesongs.blogspot.com in the August 14th and 15th entries of 2020.

Page 24: That also happened to me – as soon as I wrote down the song, I heard these 2 owls hooting – they really were harmonizing with each other. It felt like some kind of magic was happening there.

Page 25: The picture in the middle is the one I used when I posted the song on the blog. The picture and the song both have banjos in them – and I realized after the fact, whoah, the old lady – who gave me a song about a circle – also plays a circular instrument (a banjo). That's wild. The song, itself, is about how I like Linkin Park – how they're the band that does it for me, and as such complete a gestalt for me – the same way a circle is a gestalt. But it's a bluegrassy song, so it doesn't actually sound like Linkin Park.

Page 26: I'd smoked some pot one night and was thinking about how we might be where England was a year ago. It tripped me out. I wasn't as tripped out the next day, though, but occasionally, I'll get tripped out when I think about that stuff.

Page 27: The "rolling through town" dude came in a dream the same night I'd gotten baked and had the above insight. The dude was all excited in the dream about moving through space, even when staying subjectively still. Like, the dude is staying still, but he ends up where the town he's rolling through was a few minutes ago because of the earth's rotation putting him there.

Page 28: The thing with the ball bouncing around is from an actual dream. A person was talking about this medical treatment that involved a giant beach ball bouncing around a parking lot and then the ball went crazy. I started to wonder if the ball was a metaphor for the ego.

I didn't initially like one of the drawings of me at the bottom, but changed my mind about it later. The one with the wrong nose was what I was gonna cut and paste on top of the original image when I scanned the page into the computer. But then I changed my mind and decided I liked the original one. So, I made the two girls facing the camera as being mirror images of each other.

Page 29: Yeah, I'd tripped myself up with the drawings a few pages back and was really scared I was gonna all of a sudden lose my mojo for doing these drawings, like what happened in 2011. I had no idea how the other characters were gonna respond to my freak-out in the comic strip – their staying calm surprised me in real life. When they offered the solution of making fucked up owls, that alleviated my fears. Like, the worst that can happen is I draw fucked up owls or a while – I can deal with that.

Page 30: Yeah, I'd been feeling like the drawings I did of the old lady with a banjo didn't really capture her essence the way I wanted them to. I always imagined her as being more joyful – like, super, super joyful and not all inhibited. For some reason, making her a mirror image of myself made it feel less disrespectful than otherwise. I'm not sure why that is. Maybe since I'm making myself look the same, it's like, "Hey, it's okay, old lady with the banjo, cuz I look that way, too!"

I also wonder – she's my ancestor (at least, I think she is). In a sense, she does live inside me cuz we share the same DNA. I probably have some ancestral memories kicking around in me that are hers, as well. In a sense, we are the same. I also believe we're connected to our ancestors on a spiritual level – it's almost like, when I look at a mirror – any time I look at a mirror – I'm looking at my ancestors.

Page 31: The stuff about the fire is real – the sweat lodge I used to go to really did burn down in the fire in the Santa Cruz mountains. Then I speak to my continued wanting to believe that horrible-awful-bad things can't happen, like those beautiful redwood trees burning down. It's weird, cuz even though I know, first hand, that bad things happen, it's still hard for me to believe.

The Starbucks is a reference to Volume 1 of the Adventures of Jesus and Chief Running Dog – Chief Running Dog discovers, to his chagrin, that he and Jesus (in a past life), as well as his friends and ancestors were buried where a Starbucks now stands.

Page 32: Dang, that was a major big thing in my internal explorations, the making of this page. It kinda made all the puzzle pieces come together as to why I'm drawn to indigenous culture, while also wanting to connect with my own ancestors. I hear that country music is what Celtic music became when Europeans came over here. It feels like country music is that bridge between me (here on this land) and my European ancestors. There's something so beautiful that I can't describe about that discovery o' mine, that country music is intimately connected to me and my ancestors. I've been recording a lot more country songs lately, as a result of this discovery.

Page 33: Then something really bad happened, the bad thing I referred to earlier in this notes section. It makes me sad – I was only 2 pages away from ending this book, and it ended up not having a happy ending, cuz I was in a poopy-bad place when I did these last 2 pages. And yet, there's something beautiful about me askin' if the universe makes mistakes and if I'm one of them. I dunno why it strikes me as beautiful (it sorta seems like it shouldn't), but it does. It almost makes me think of what people might say in a really deep and super-sad European movie or something.

The bad thing that happened made me feel like I'm a mistake. But I'm gonna keep on living anyway, cuz maybe I'm not a mistake. Maybe. And even if I am a mistake, I might be a mistake that leads to good stuff. Maybe. Maybe.

Page 34: Country music is a balm, and a salve, for these lives that get poopy. It keeps us going. Our lives got sad when we went from bein' indigenous to not being indigenous. Country music knew it was gonna happen, knew we were gonna get sad, and it was there to help. Thank you, country music.

The black woman says to keep goin'. That's what I plan to do. This work is some of the important-est work of my life. I'm gonna keep at it.